MW01009425

PRAISE FOR
INTENTION IMPERATIVE

"Mark Sanborn has done it again! Just as his past bestsellers have done, *The Intention Imperative* covers new ground in arming today's leaders with valuable, relevant insight. In his creative, straightforward style, Mark details how elements like clarity, purpose, meaning, and intent have never been more critical than they are right now. This book should be required reading for every business leader navigating the modern workplace."

—ADAM CONTOS,
CEO, RE/MAX Holdings, Inc.

"Mark Sanborn goes beyond writing purely about effective leadership and focuses on intentional leadership. One follows common definitions; the other creates and inspires new approaches to successful leadership in fast-changing environments."

—TODD WANEK,
CEO, Ashley Furniture Industries

"You'll enjoy studying this book on intentional leadership. It shows how successful leaders create capacity in their associates and grow organizations ethically and congruently."

—MICHAEL T. LAWTON,
former CFO, Domino's Pizza, Inc.

"This book is a must-read for anyone leading a team, guiding the culture of their organization, or coaching others. It's substantive and inspiring."

—JANET KERR,
Vice Chancellor, Pepperdine University

"Intentional leaders are positive disruptors creating the transformational shifts that need to happen both now and in the future. Find out how by reading this important and timely book today!"

—DANIEL BURRUS,
author of the *New York Times* bestseller *Flash Foresight,*
and his latest bestseller, *The Anticipatory Organization*

"Mark's examples of Intentional Leadership are inspiring and profound. I can't wait to share this book with my team!"

—MARK EASON,
CEO, Firebirds Wood Fired Grill

"Every entrepreneur in America should read *The Intention Imperative*. Filled with innovative but practical tactics that you can implement immediately, this book will be required reading for all my coaching clients."

—MARTY GRUNDER,
CEO, Grunder Landscaping;
President and CEO, The Grow Group

THE
INTENTION
IMPERATIVE

3 Essential Changes That Will Make You a Successful Leader Today

MARK SANBORN

HARPERCOLLINS
LEADERSHIP

AN IMPRINT OF HARPERCOLLINS

To the leaders I've had the privilege to serve in my career:
thank you for your interest, your support,
and your commitment to lead well.

The Intention Imperative

© 2019 by Mark Sanborn

All rights reserved. No portion of this book may be reproduced, stored in a retrieval system, or transmitted in any form or by any means—electronic, mechanical, photocopy, recording, scanning, or other—except for brief quotations in critical reviews or articles, without the prior written permission of the publisher.

Published by HarperCollins Leadership, an imprint of HarperCollins Focus LLC.
Published in association with Yates & Yates, www.yates2.com.

Book design by Maria Fernandez, Neuwirth & Associates.

Any internet addresses, phone numbers, or company or product information printed in this book are offered as a resource and are not intended in any way to be or to imply an endorsement by HarperCollins Leadership, nor does HarperCollins Leadership vouch for the existence, content, or services of these sites, phone numbers, companies, or products beyond the life of this book.
Unless otherwise noted, quotations in this book were taken from personal interviews with business professionals between 2018 and 2019.

ISBN 978-0-7180-9317-4 (Ebook)
ISBN 978-0-7180-9315-0 (HC)

Library of Congress Cataloging-in-Publication Data

Names: Sanborn, Mark, author.
Title: The intention imperative : 3 essential changes that will make you a successful leader today / Mark Sanborn.
Description: Nashville: HarperCollins Leadership, [2019]
Identifiers: LCCN 2019009312 (print) | LCCN 2019011183 (ebook) | ISBN 9780718093174 (e-book) | ISBN 9780718093150 (hardcover)
Subjects: LCSH: Leadership. | Success.
Classification: LCC HD57.7 (ebook) | LCC HD57.7 .S256 2019 (print) | DDC 658.4/092--dc23
LC record available at https://lccn.loc.gov/2019009312

Printed in the United States of America

19 20 21 22 23 LSC 10 9 8 7 6 5 4 3 2 1

CONTENTS

CHAPTER 1

A QUESTION I COULDN'T ANSWER

What's the one thing all successful leaders have in common?
For thirty years, I have been asked this question and for thirty years I didn't have a satisfactory answer. I could have made something up, but it wouldn't have been honest or valid. Leadership, after all, is a special combination of unique qualities, the balance of which is as varied as the leaders themselves.

In leadership development, generalities come to mind: leaders are inspirational, focused, innovative, brilliant, and sometimes a little crazy. But do any of these characteristics rise above the others?

Was Henry Ford more innovative than focused?

Was Steve Jobs more brilliant than inspirational?

Ask a hundred people and you'll get a hundred answers. The reality of this leads to two possible conclusions: (1) the question itself is rather useless, because *no one thing* defines a great leader, or (2) a singular identification of the one thing great leaders have in common is elusive and unknown.

The question also assumes that leadership is unchanging, that what made Ford a great leader isn't so much different from what made Jobs one as well. As we'll see, I do believe there is truth to the universality of leadership, but I remain skeptical that a resurrected Ford, without a penny to his name, could repeat his stupendous success in the twenty-first century—or that a time-traveling Jobs would be smoking cigars with the robber barons of the nineteenth century. Not to take anything away from either leader, but things *have changed and continue to change*.

For these reasons, I have been honest when asked this question: I don't know that "one thing" all great leaders share. I know leaders who did nearly everything right but who were remarkably mediocre in the results they achieved. I also know leaders who did a lot wrong but were able to achieve amazing results. Then, to confound things even further, I have known leaders who have achieved both amazing success and terrific failure. Same leaders, wildly different results.

Then I had an epiphany: no one ends up at the top of Mount Everest accidentally.

The defining characteristic that all successful leaders have in common is *intentionality*. In other words, a climber takes consistent action to get to the top of the world. Likewise, great leaders act consistently to achieve their goals. Mediocre leaders might have a goal but act inconsistently to get there. Then there are the bad leaders, those with no goal and no consistent action.

The difference between the three is dramatic.

For a while I was happy with this breakthrough. My other theories and notions on leadership started to spin around this central core, like planets around the sun. But something still seemed to be missing. Is being intentional all it takes?

Turns out, no. There's more to leadership than intentionality.

At a gathering of small- to medium-size companies in Phoenix in 2016, a group of four of my closest friends and I led a session on helping these owners and leaders grow their businesses. Formally, this group was known as the Five Friends, all of us bestselling authors, speakers, business consultants, and, yes, great friends as well. It became clear that despite the diversity of businesses in the room, most faced a common challenge, and it wasn't intentionality. This was a group that was intentional. These were high achievers. But they still needed help—as many leaders do—in one area. What was that one area?

I'll get to that area in a minute, because it is essential to what I call intentional leadership. Intentionality, it turns out, is worthless without it. And I've come to believe that intentionality is inextricably intertwined with it. And, after thirty years of thought and study, I can now answer the question of what all great leadership has in common.

THE PARAMETERS OF GREAT LEADERSHIP

But before answering the question, we first need to set some boundaries. The type of leadership I'm talking about is organizational in general but business-oriented in particular. I do believe that the answer applies to any type of leadership, from political to military to industry, but to entertain these other areas would be to write a book without much focus. (And, as we'll see in a moment, focus is no small thing when it comes to great leadership.) Effective leaders in every arena, in ages past and present, have something to tell us, and I will "cheat" and use some of their insights and ideas to highlight and support the assertions and insights that follow in this book. Nevertheless, the practical application of my lessons is intended for those who lead organizations in the world of business.

Second, let's avoid the anomalies. One can always think of some lucky flukes or one-hit wonders who caught the proverbial lightning in a bottle. Good for them. I don't wish to take away from their accomplishments, but I want to focus on those leaders who have exhibited sustainable and replicable success. I'm not going to let the one-offs derail leadership lessons in this book.

Third, profitability isn't the sole consideration of a great leader. It is a primary one, to be sure, because without profit a business wouldn't exist. But if money was all that mattered, then we would be ignoring other essential components of great leadership. Uber founder and CEO Travis Kalanick built an extremely profitable company that will go down as one of the most disruptive in history. He was also fired for having nurtured a destructive workplace culture. Uber (and Kalanick) should be commended for many things—leadership isn't one of them.

Next, let's discuss failure. Failure doesn't necessarily mean bad leadership. In fact, navigating a company through failure is one of the hallmarks of a great leader. And few leaders are uniformly successful through their careers. They experience setbacks and failures like the rest of us. The net effect, however, is one of success.

But we must consider the source and magnitude of the failure when judging a leader. The definitions I provide in this book look at leadership from several angles, but they add up to a complete whole. To have built an outstanding culture in a business whose product failed to sell is like defaulting on a beautiful home you purchased.

Finally, as much as possible, I'm going to focus on the present day. As we'll see, an essential component of great leadership involves working in the world *as it is*. Leadership doesn't exist in a vacuum. This is truer than ever, as the ever-changing state of technology and the pressure this puts on the modern business are more profound than at any time in history. This doesn't mean that the great leaders of the past have nothing to tell us, but it does mean that leadership, as I define it, is inseparable from the world in which the leader lives and works.

In practice, what this means is that I'll avoid regurgitating stories about Henry Ford or Steve Jobs.

CLIMBING MOUNT EVEREST

Now back to Everest and the insight that fired my imagination in Phoenix.

To reach the summit of the tallest mountain in the world is one of humanity's great achievements. Even if the occasional amateur climber does make the top, that climber doesn't do so without a great deal of determination, extensive planning and preparation, and sustained effort. There's no other way to get there. To summit Everest requires a mental focus and physical endurance that is simply beyond the scope of most people. You can't do it on a whim. In fact, you can die if you aren't 100 percent committed to the goal (and even the 100 percent committed sometimes die anyway).

To repeat: no one reaches the top of Mount Everest accidentally.

In Phoenix, I contemplated the common challenges of our clients and listened to them to determine what else, aside from intentionality, is a necessary component of great leadership. Many of the people in the room that day were torn, not sure exactly what it was they really wanted to do. Some were chasing more than one rabbit and catching none. Others were trying lots of different things, not just in the spirit of innovation but because they weren't sure what they really wanted to do, what they should do, or what they could do. And in that discussion lay the answer.

The first thing one would need to climb Mount Everest is *clarity*.

Put another way: *What do you want to do?* Answer: *I want to climb Mount Everest.* Simple. Direct. Precise. It's a goal that doesn't need qualifications or further explanation. It's a goal that has only two possible outcomes: either you stand on the top of the world or you don't. Yes, there are details—hundreds, if not thousands, of little devils and considerations that will determine your success in this endeavor. But, as a goal, it doesn't get any clearer than this: *I* am *going to climb Mount Everest.*

No one who has done anything great did it by chance. Shakespeare didn't write *Hamlet* by chance, Michelangelo didn't end up with the Sistine Chapel, and Neil Armstrong didn't suddenly find himself on the moon. Each one achieved greatness starting from a single point: clarity of vision, of goal, of purpose. They knew exactly where they wanted to go. People do win the lottery, but no one creates greatness just by buying a random ticket.

And if greatness doesn't happen by chance, neither does great business leadership. When I applied this idea of clarity to the thousands of clients with whom I've worked over the years in nearly every imaginable market space, I saw the difference between the mediocre and the great: clarity. The great ones knew where they wanted to go; the mediocre ones kinda had an idea. Many had no idea at all. With clarity, everything works. Without it, nothing works.

What does clarity look like when it comes to a business leader? I asked that very question of Jesse Cole, whom you'll get to know much better later on. Here's what he said: "The name of our company is Fans First Entertainment. Our mission is 'Fans First. Entertain Always.' *We believe we can provide the best fan experience in the world.* That's what we want to be known for and it's what we stand for."[1]

Simple. Direct. Precise. Above all, clear.

Clarity is the starting point. The great leaders of business began with a clear understanding of where they wanted to go, what they wanted to build, whom they wanted to serve. They could explain what success looks like, what their version of standing atop the world would be.

Can you?

CLARITY ABOUT WHAT?

Let's be honest. Isn't clarity just a fancy way of saying what your company does? If you're in the business of making furniture, then what else do you need to be clear about? You want to sell as much furniture as you can. There, that's clarity!

Except it's not. You might as well say that you just want to make as much money as you can, all else be damned. To define your goal in terms of sales isn't a goal. Yes, everyone is in the business of making money—but that's also the point. *Everyone* is in the business of making money. I can't say how IKEA founder Ingvar Kamprad would have defined his Mount Everest, but I'm pretty sure it wasn't just to sell a lot of furniture.

Why do I know this?

Because he never said anything of the sort during his time leading IKEA to be the world's largest furniture retailer and becoming a self-made billionaire in the process. Here's what he did say, however:

> "Our idea is to serve everybody, including people with little money."

> "To do business with a clear conscience is an attitude that pays. We have to find more time for ourselves and to regain respect for the environment in which we live."

> "If there is such a thing as good leadership, it is to give a good example. I have to do so for all the IKEA employees."[2]

These are the words of a leader who knew there was more to his business than selling a lot of furniture. He had a vision of what his company was supposed to be, how it was supposed to serve its customers, and how he, as its leader, was supposed to show the way. Obviously, there's so much more that goes into what made Kamprad an exceptional leader, but it all begins with the clarity he had for his business and for himself.

How can you help achieve your own clarity? I'm glad you asked. You can begin with some simple questions:

- What do we aspire to do?
- Why do we want to do it?
- How do our people feel about doing it?
- How does the customer feel about what we do?
- How does our culture create and expedite doing it?
- Finally, are all of the above congruent and in alignment?

If you can't answer these questions, then you are a long way from achieving clarity. As you can see, not one of the questions talks about sales.

Additionally, I have very good reasons for why I chose questions that focus not just on what your organization does but also on who your customers are and on what your culture is like. For now, answer these as best you can.

Next, it's time to look inward. We're talking about leadership after all, so we should look at the leader:

- Why do I lead?
- What kind of leader do I want to be?
- How will I keep getting better?
- How will I last?

Whether you can answer all or only some of these questions, you'll immediately notice that your responses combined add up to a little more than "I want to climb Mount Everest." Isn't clarity supposed to be simple? Shouldn't I be able to distill everything down to one bumper sticker–size line? Ideally, yes, but we're a long way from understanding the purpose of clarity as a tool to guide you and your organization toward greatness. These are the baby steps, and more will be revealed.

More importantly, I can guarantee that the answers you give to these questions *now* won't look anything like the answers you will give *after finishing this book*. Don't worry so much about that. It's enough to spend just a little bit of time answering these questions as honestly—and in as many words—as you can. Believe me, if you do that, you'll be doing more than most business leaders have ever done.

FIRST PRINCIPLES

But if your answers are going to change, then why go through the exercise at all? Because I want you to read this book with some first principles in mind—for yourself and for your organization. When we begin to clarify our purpose, we begin to simplify. We begin to distill our wishes, desires, plans, and goals for ourselves and for our organization down to their essentials. We can call these essentials our first principles. What do we want to do and what do we believe? The ability to define first principles is, as Aristotle observed thousands of years ago, "the first basis from which a thing is known."[3] This "thing" is your business.

Life can be very complicated. And running a business sometimes feels like trying to change the tire on a moving car. But when a leader starts with clarity, when she knows where the car is headed, then she can begin to simplify the choices before her. If your goal is to climb Everest, then everything you do either puts you closer to that goal or takes you further away. Yes, easier said than done, particularly when dealing with a modern-day company. *Will* pursuing this market get us closer to our goal? *Should* we revamp our sales funnel? So many questions, so little clarity.

But the identification of first principles, which are like a proven route on your trek up the mountain, helps the great leader navigate through the foggy conditions and uncertainty about what's around the next bend. It is very hard to change course once you are headed in the wrong direction. But at least you *know* you're going in the wrong direction. Most leaders don't know. The aspirations you have for your organization can be compared to the reality of your situation. Are they aligned or are they unbalanced?

We aren't looking for the final answers just yet. But if we can establish a baseline, then what follows will be that much more effective in helping you achieve true clarity.

INTENTIONALITY AND CLARITY—
A COMBUSTIBLE MIX

So now we have the defining characteristics of great leadership: clarity and intentionality. The first, clarity, tells you where you're headed. You're at base camp looking up at the summit. You gather your team and point: "That's where we're going."

The second, intentionality, is the consistent action you'll take to get there. For the mountain climber, it's a series of acclimatization climbs, preparing the body for ever-higher altitudes, followed by the beginning of the trek, moving from base camp up the mountain. *Everything* the team does from the moment the leader points at the summit is directed toward achieving that goal.

Together, these two ideas are the basic elements a leader needs to navigate his business toward greatness. Yet I realize that that still isn't much of an answer. A couple of vague terms, loosely connected? How does that help you? Not much, but it's a start.

CHAPTER 2

INTENTIONAL LEADERSHIP, DEFINED

W hat's your favorite pizza? I bet it isn't Domino's. Yet did you know that since 2008, Domino's stock has risen 5,000 percent?[1] 5,000 percent.

How in the world does a company that makes mediocre pizza see that type of success?

Two words: intentional leadership.

Here's a very brief history of Domino's, just to catch you up. In the 2000s, the franchise company that revolutionized—no, all but invented—the home-delivery model had hit hard times. The product was, by the company's own admission, lousy. In fact, toward the end of the decade, Domino's began running commercials admitting that its pizza was pretty terrible—or at least that customers thought it was pretty terrible. But so what? Domino's is about convenience. No one expects to get the best pizza when they call in an order.

But the decline of quality certainly played a role. When a consumer in the 2000s wanted to order a pizza, she had plenty of options. She could pay a little more for local or call up one of many franchise businesses like Papa John's. The point is that nothing about Domino's stood out anymore. Everyone provided home delivery, which meant Domino's was competing on quality—not its strong suit.

By 2008, during the height of the Great Recession, Domino's stock was a record-low three dollars a share. Two years later, J. Patrick Doyle, who had been with the company since 1997, was made CEO, and things began to change. The first thing to happen was that the company revamped the way it made pizza. The commercials mentioned above were part of raising awareness for the new Domino's recipe, but of course they made a marketing splash by admitting wrongdoing.

Producing better pizza wasn't the whole solution. How could it be? At the end of the day, Domino's still faced an avalanche of competition, and there is a ceiling of how good a pizza can be at such a low cost. More had to be done, but what?

As recounted in an article in *Forbes*, the top leadership gathered for a meeting in 2012 to go over the extent of the problems facing the company, which were monumental. There was a breakthrough. Or, perhaps it's better to say, they finally had some clarity. And they found it by asking a simple question:

What kind of company are we?

Their answer: "An e-commerce company that happens to sell pizza."[2]

Why was this such a groundbreaking insight? Because you'll notice that pizza is relegated to the second position. Domino's realized that its customers knew it didn't have the best pizza. But it also understood that they didn't want—or expect—the best pizza. What they wanted was convenience, efficiency, and cost-effectiveness. That's what e-commerce delivers, no pun intended. Customers don't order Domino's to impress; they order it so that they can spend their time on other activities.

The main result of this epiphany was a devotion to the company's technology side, namely, its app. The Domino's app would end up pioneering technology that many smartphone users take for granted today, such as mobile payments. The company designed a user experience that blew away the competition, making ordering a fast, fresh pizza as simple as a few clicks. And I do mean a few clicks. If you go with the app's "Your Easy Order," you can have a pizza at your door in fewer than five taps on your screen. One of the most distinctive features of the app is the order tracker, which gives users updates on where their pizza is at any given moment—in the oven, out of the oven, or out for delivery. It's like a UPS package tracker on steroids, and it is little wonder that competitors like Pizza Hut have copied it. The company also expanded into voice recognition technology and ordering through Twitter.[3]

You get the point. Today, Domino's stock hovers around $250 a share. Remarkable, right? But perhaps the more telling stat is that Domino's has outperformed all the world's largest tech companies this decade. Yes, that includes Google, Amazon, Facebook, and Apple.[4] Granted, Domino's climbed out of a pretty deep hole, but no one could have predicted that a pizza company would be on the same level as Silicon Valley.

And yet that's where Domino's knew it had to be. How it got there was through intentional leadership.

INTENTIONALITY MEETS CLARITY

The story of Domino's incredible turnaround has been told many times before. A 2016 article in the *Harvard Business Review* was titled "How Domino's Pizza Reinvented Itself." You see this idea of reinvention pop up a lot in stories about Domino's, but to me this misses the point. Domino's didn't reinvent itself. A reinvention would have been if Domino's had started selling Chinese food or smartphones. Rather, Domino's returned to its roots. It's not doing anything fundamentally different today from what it did in the 1980s.

But let's look at Domino's success through the lens of intentional leadership. To do that we need to rephrase the premise: Domino's didn't become a successful e-commerce company that happens to sell pizza *accidentally*. That was its stated intention; that was its Mount Everest. It was *clear* about what it wanted to be.

Now, let's go back one step further. How did the company know what it wanted to be? By returning to its first principles. Domino's was never about making the best pizza; it was about delivering a good pizza very quickly. There was an era when this and this alone was a huge competitive advantage. But as time went by, this advantage dwindled until Domino's was just one of many companies delivering good food fast. It's a reality that still exists today. How could Domino's stand out?

By doing what it did in its infancy: by being faster than the other guy. This has always been Domino's first principle and one that helped it see where it wanted to go, to see the top of its own Everest.

Now, to intentionality: *How* can Domino's be faster? Or, how do we get to the top of Mount Everest? What consistent action could Domino's take to reach its stated ambition?

Answer: e-commerce. Who would have thought that consumers were tired of picking up a phone and giving an operator an order? I mean, why should a company invest precious resources improving on that? It is what it is. Yet Domino's was able to see what its competitors didn't: the advent of smartphones had intensified the interaction between consumer and company.

Why go to a restaurant when you can order takeout?

Why order takeout when you can order delivery?

Why pick up a phone to have it delivered when you can tap it into your smartphone?

The Domino's app, and much of the company's subsequent online offerings, didn't just follow where other industries had led—it created the tools that other industries now use. And it's hard to see how any of this would have happened had Domino's not matched its clarity with its intentionality.

If Domino's had seen itself as a pizza company that happened to deliver, then it would have focused on the quality of its pizza above all else. I don't mean to suggest that quality was unimportant in Domino's turnaround. After all, it did spend millions of marketing dollars telling the world that Domino's pizza would be better. Also, if Domino's hadn't intentionally climbed the mountain through the pathway of e-commerce, then it might have returned to its old "thirty minutes or your pizza is free" gimmick from decades earlier. Indeed, Domino's, as a case study in intentional leadership, shows why it's critical to not only know where you want to go but how you want to get there.

Of course Domino's knew where it wanted to go, because it had already been there. By returning to first principles, it knew why customers had once trusted them as their primary pizza-delivery service. But the coup de grâce was in seeing more clearly than its competition that the way up the mountain had changed.

FOUR TYPES OF LEADERSHIP

So, we have further defined intentional leadership as a combination of intentionality and clarity. To put it in plain terms: know where you want to go (clarity), and take consistent action on how you want to get there (intentionality). You discover where you want to go through a firm understanding of your first principles: what you believe in as a company and what value you bring to customers. You find out how you want to get there by looking at the world *as it is*. In the case of Domino's, the world *as it is* was very different from the world *that was* when it exploded on the scene in the 1980s. We'll discuss in greater detail the concept of the world *as it is* in chapter 4.

For now, let's further explore the interplay between intentionality and clarity. Not every company can point to a turnaround quite as stunning as Domino's. In fact, few can. Most muddy their way through, doing their best not to fall off the mountain. So it's best to begin by looking at where leaders go wrong in navigating their way up to the summit:

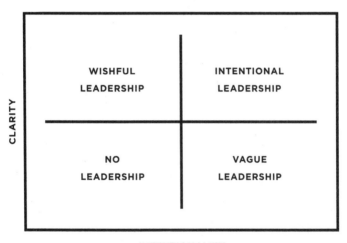

The Four Types of Leadership image illustrates the integral connection between clarity and intentionality, of knowing where you want to go and consistently taking the right action to get there. Obviously, you want to find yourself in the upper right quadrant, benefiting from the power of intentional leadership alongside other great companies like Domino's. But honestly, where are you? Might you find yourself in one of the other three quadrants, not necessarily failing but also not reaching the summit of your particular Mount Everest?

Let's take a look at each quadrant individually. Perhaps you'll see where you are at this moment:

> *No Leadership*: A lack of clarity and intentionality equals a lack of leadership. At the very least, a leader must convey to his team a direction, a point on the horizon toward which they must all steer the ship. Failure to do so is negligence and likely will lead to either the loss of your leadership position or failure of the company (and maybe both). How do you know if you're in this category? Easy. Answer these two questions:

> 1. Do you know where you want to go?
> 2. Are you driving the appropriate action to get there?

Now present the same two questions to the members of your executive team. You might know the answers, but if they don't, then you're still stuck in the worst quadrant. You also might hear different answers depending on whom you ask, which is another red flag.

In my experience, more companies find themselves in this quadrant than you might expect. If nothing changes, then the end is certainly near, but a lot of companies are able to tread water for a long time before slipping under the waves. The good news is that you'll probably know if you're in this quadrant, because things will not be going well.

Or you'll be fired.

> *Vague Leadership:* You embrace the concept of "ready, fire, aim." You constantly introduce bold new initiatives. You have a bias for action. You want your teams in high gear, and every person in every department must be busy.

Some leaders think they can achieve greatness simply by setting lofty goals. Others don't set any goals at all, aside from some vague directive to increase sales. Either way, your chances of reaching the summit are low indeed if you're not taking the right and consistent actions to get there.

The problem is you and the members of your team aren't sure where you are going or—if you think you know—why you are going there at all.

Your road map to success looks more like a Chinese puzzle . . . viewed from the inside of a maze.

While luck favors momentum, you want more than luck on your side. You want a clear view of your reason for being and your primary goals. You want to answer the *what* and the *why* of what you're about before you get the *how* into high gear. Vague leadership results in false starts, in wasted resources and energy. Worse, there's a very good chance you'll end up where you don't want to be.

> *Wishful Leadership*: If you're in this quadrant, you know where you want to go, but you either haven't figured out how to get there or you aren't taking consistent action to do so. You want to climb Mount Everest but you haven't taken climbing lessons, or if you once took them, you're not practicing what you learned.

Wishful leadership also lacks a compelling purpose. The need for clarity is driven by fear of failure or increased marketplace demands, but it isn't coupled with effective action. And sometimes wishful leaders try to do too much. It's as if Domino's had wanted to have the best pizza, at the best price, with the best customer experience. You can't have all three, but the fantasy leader divides his team's resources and energies toward creating the best of three. Which is how you get the best of none.

The wishful leader listens to his experts, takes lots of notes, convenes many meetings, but then never drives for completed action. Information gathering substitutes for action taking. The inundation of information can be paralyzing, particularly in this day and age when Big Data seems to be driving every business decision.

Wishful leadership also happens when leaders chase the market. Clarity changes frequently and often dramatically. Domino's decided to do an app because it was the best way to achieve greater intimacy with their customers. Another company outside the food industry might look at Domino's success and say, "We need an app too!"

Why?

The leader can't say. She only knows that the company needs one *because everyone else has one.* Just because everyone else has an app doesn't mean you should spend time and resources developing one.

Intentional Leadership: How you get to this quadrant will occupy the rest of this book. But we can now give a better definition than what you've read so far:

Intentional leadership is knowing where you want to go and taking consistent action in the world as it is, not in the world that was, to get there.

I relied on Domino's to exemplify this definition, but only as a way to introduce you to these fundamental concepts using a well-known success story. The broad strokes I used to illustrate intentional leadership will now start to become finer. It's time to dig down to find the raw materials. The world *as it is* has placed demands on today's leader that have radically changed the game. You've likely seen these ideas discussed elsewhere—ideas like culture, inspiration, and the ever-changing economy. What you probably haven't seen is *how* these three forces connect, because they all feed into one another. And it's at their point of intersection that we find the heart of true business leadership in today's world.

And now it's time for you to meet Bob and Gloria.

CHAPTER 3

A TALE OF TWO LEADERS

Bob inherited his father's parking garage in a busy downtown neighborhood. For years, business was good and Bob was able to keep his lot at capacity and prices low enough that nobody complained. Bob's luck ran out, however, when a new garage was built across the street. The new lot's owner, Gloria, had different ideas about how to manage a parking garage. Apparently, the parking-garage industry is small and word spreads quickly. Bob heard about Gloria's new ideas and laughed.

"She won't last a year," he mused.

This is the story of how two parking-garage owners saw their roles very differently. It is a story of leadership in an industry where leadership seems like too fancy a word. Bob didn't see himself as a "leader." He owned a parking garage! The world might have changed radically in those decades, but parking? Parking was the same as it ever was. Be mindful of the competition, keep your garage clean and safe, and compete on price.

In other words, stay the course—that was Bob's vision.

But Gloria came from retail, and she had a different perspective. The world *had* changed and it affected everything and everyone. Gloria believed she owned more than a concrete structure that housed cars. She believed her few employees were more than parking attendants.

Gloria had every intention of being a leader. Let them laugh. She would have the last one.

EXPERIENCE WORKS—UNTIL IT DOESN'T

With decades of experience behind him, Bob knew the parking-garage business better than anyone. He could rattle off parking-lot data and formulas like a professor in front of a classroom. He knew how to keep his garage packed. He knew how to get them in and out quickly and efficiently. Most of all, he knew how to keep his costs down and his prices low.

"Beat 'em on price," his father would always say. All of Bob's experience told him that the parking-garage business depended on two things, and only two things: location and price. The better the location, the higher the price. Which meant that if Bob could undercut his competition, then he would win more customers.

Although Bob saw the changes in the world around him, he never imagined they affected his garage. The pace of business had certainly shifted. Things happened faster than when he was working under his father. The internet had affected the way customers found his garage, but Bob made sure his garage was on all the right search engines. The moment someone in the area used their phone to look for a place to park, Bob's garage came right up.

Barring some future time when people didn't drive cars to work anymore, Bob was confident that the world wasn't all that much different from when his father ran things and would remain that way. His customers needed a place to park: Bob provided a place to park. Simple. Easy. A dummy could do this.

Bob didn't really think in terms of clarity and intentionality. What was the point? But if he had to express his vision for his parking garage, he probably would say something along the lines of "We give customers a place to park their cars cheaply." That about summed up Bob's vision.

Gloria's experience came from retail, where she knew that customers expected a more intimate, more personal connection with companies. They expected a service tailored to their preferences. If Amazon could send them suggestions based off their purchase and search history, then why couldn't other retailers? If customers were going to provide their email, then they expected tangible results—like discounts, suggestions based on their purchase and viewing habits, and early access to in-demand products.

To the outside observer, none of this has anything to do with parking garages. But to Gloria, her experience in other industries told her that no company exists in a vacuum. To believe that an industry is somehow impervious to the gargantuan changes going on around it is naïveté of the first order. The question Gloria had was: How did this new world affect parking garages? She knew it had to; her job was to find out how.

As opposed to Bob, Gloria did have a vision for her company. She wrote it down when she was putting together her plan. It went something like this: "A parking garage that served customers with the best experience possible." Furthermore, she laid out how she would get there, and, tellingly, none of it mentioned price. First, she would focus on her employees . . . wait, what? How many employees does a parking garage need? We'll get to that, but Gloria believed that by creating the conditions in which her employees could thrive, she would be laying the foundation for a business that customers would want to frequent. Second, she wanted her team to know that they were decidedly *not* in the "parking cars" business. Instead, they were in the business of serving people. It sounds trite, but Gloria wanted to hammer home the point with her employees that *her* garage would offer more than just a space to park a car. Finally, she believed she could upend the model that guided all of Bob's strategic thinking. Yes, the garage industry depended on location and price. But Gloria's instinct told her that customers didn't just expect goods or services in exchange for money anymore. That was the old world. Today, customers expected a good experience. She wanted her customers to feel good about leaving their cars in her care.

Two different worldviews, two different backgrounds, and two very different ways of doing business. Everything that Bob knew about parking garages was working against him. Everything that Gloria had learned about the way customers interacted with companies was about to pay off.

IMAGINATION, NOT AUTOMATION

It's not that Bob was against newer ways of doing things. For years, he had relied on a handful of human cashiers to pass out tickets upon entry and take customers' payment upon exit. But Bob couldn't ignore the long-term savings of investing in machines, and so he happily replaced employees with automation. He was pleased that he could cut his workforce (and his expenses) down to a bare minimum, and he knew his customers would appreciate the faster check-out times. Win-win. From the moment someone entered Bob's garage to the moment they left, Bob hoped they wouldn't encounter a single employee. It was a smooth, efficient operation that held to a simple philosophy: get in, get out, get on with your life.

Gloria had other ideas. She *wanted* her customers to interact with her employees. Does that mean she kept human-operated ticket and pay-ment booths? Certainly not. She installed the machines just like every other garage. But she nevertheless wanted a human on every floor of her garage, not just for safety matters but also to be on hand to answer customer questions and concerns. In other words, she wanted customer-service representatives to be in the "front of the house," as they say in the restaurant industry. That also meant she needed to hire far more deliberately than most garages probably do. She wanted her employees to be personable, knowledgeable, and accessible.

But Gloria's vision had one problem. The sort of person she wanted working for her probably isn't looking to get into the parking-garage industry. Who wants to spend their days in a dark garage full of fumes? If she wanted to build a business focused on people, then she first had to take care of her own. That meant investing in facilities that would reduce or eliminate the otherwise normal "garage feel." They couldn't be expected to work in a run-down, makeshift room. They had to have an office that was inviting and welcoming to both employees and customers alike.

Above all, Gloria had to create a working environment in which her team members felt as if they worked for a real company, one that valued them as employees and individuals, one that treated them with dignity and respect, and one that allowed them to grow their skills. Bob looked at employees as necessary costs, which is why he was so happy to strip his workforce down to the bare minimum. Gloria, however, saw employees as her greatest asset. And to get the best, she needed to invest.

A COMPANY FOR PEOPLE, NOT CARS

When one of Bob's few employees showed up for work each day, he went straight to his little room in the corner of one of the garage floors. He took an hour for lunch, then went back to his desk. Maybe he helped a customer fix their flat tire (if asked) or worked out some problems with the automated payment machines. But for the most part, Bob's employees spent their days alone. The job wasn't too difficult and perhaps they enjoyed not being hassled all day long. They rarely met the "boss," who almost never visited the garage except during emergencies. Bob didn't expect much from his workers, who, in turn, didn't ask for much. Everyone was content.

Gloria expected more from her employees. But she also knew that if you want more from your team, you need to give them more in return—and not just financial incentives. With her retail background, Gloria knew that the best employees are those who love their job, the ones who got a kick out of helping the customers, who felt good at the end of the day. If she wanted her garage to compete on more than just price and location, then she needed a team that was inspired and motivated to perform their daily tasks.

But it's a garage! How in the world do you motivate them?

Much like her problem of hiring the right people, Gloria knew that to get the most out of her team, she needed to change the equation. She needed them to believe that they were part of something just a bit bigger than a place where people parked their cars. They needed to believe that they were helping someone. They needed meaning.

Gloria attacked the problem in two ways. First, she wanted to instill a sense of camaraderie in her employees, the feeling that they belonged to a team. Where Bob's employees might spend their whole day in isolation, Gloria's workers met each morning to go over the priorities of the day: What problems happened yesterday, where could they get better, and what problems might arise today? This "team huddle" was an instrumental part of the employees' day. It wasn't long or complicated, but it was necessary to get the team together, if only for a few minutes, to provide a sense of organization and community. Gloria also instituted group lunches, where employees were expected to meet in the break room to share a meal. It was a small but important step to remind the employees that they were part of something larger.

Next, Gloria instituted a training program to help the team get familiar with proper customer-service behaviors and protocols. Her team learned how to deal with angry customers, who to call for the right services, and how to go that extra mile when someone had a question or complaint. But, this being a garage after all, she also included general motor-vehicle maintenance classes so her employees could be self-sufficient in fixing common car problems. The worst thing one of Gloria's employees could do if a customer came to them with a problem was shrug their shoulders. Not at this garage! If Gloria's team couldn't fix the problem themselves, they knew exactly who could.

All of this team-building and customer-service work was put in place with a very clear goal in mind: Gloria wanted her team to stop thinking that they worked at a parking garage; she wanted them to know that they were in the business of helping others. It's one thing to say that—and Gloria certainly said that often, in person and with the company's training manuals and guidelines. But actions speak louder than words, and for Gloria, she had to have her employees learn it.

Finally, Gloria didn't just own the garage; she ran it from the premises. She had her own office in the garage and made sure to greet each employee every morning. She was also there in case customers had more urgent problems. She was visible and made sure her employees saw her do more work than they did. She was the one who taught them how to do basic automotive maintenance, she was the one who knew how to fix the ticket and payment machines, and she was the first one to admit to an aggrieved customer when something or someone didn't meet her own expectations.

If her employees were skeptical at first, they swiftly learned that Gloria was serious: this was a real company that served real people. To top it off, Gloria would ask her customers to take surveys on their experience at her garage. She used the surveys to improve the company's overall performance, but she also used them to learn which of her employees went above and beyond. Her team learned that great performance was rewarded, sometimes with recognition awards and sometimes with money. In return, Gloria got something from her employees that even the best companies and leaders value more than anything else: trust and loyalty.

A SMILE WHEN THEY LEAVE

The last part of Gloria's plan to build a different kind of parking-garage company centered on the customer experience. If her time in retail had taught Gloria one thing, it was that customers expect more than a good or service in exchange for their money—they expected a good experience. Customers gave their loyalty to companies and brands that made them feel good. The digital revolution has narrowed the gap between consumer and business to an incredibly minute degree. This has created a sense of intimacy, one which plays on a consumer's emotions. Companies have quickly learned that it's not enough to do what you'll say you'll do; you must provide an experience that leaves a smile on your customers' faces.

Bob didn't really care about his customers' experience. What kind of experience could they possibly have, after all? As long as Bob provided a safe, relatively clean garage at a reasonable price, then shouldn't they be happy? The most he did in this space was put into place a system for handling customer complaints and problems. But Bob felt that if he ever had to get personally involved with a customer, then something had broken down in the system. There was a wall between him and those who entrusted him with their cars. If the wall was breached, then Bob saw a problem.

It was exactly the opposite for Gloria, who set out to build a relationship with her customers. She wanted to know them, to learn their names, to hear their problems and their questions. Obviously, she couldn't meet everyone but Gloria made a point of walking the floors of her garage every day and stopping to talk to customers when and where she could. Most didn't care a bit about who owned the garage where they decided to park their car, but some were surprised, even amused that a garage owner would take the time to ask them if she could do anything more for them. Slowly Gloria got to know her best customers, and they started to choose Gloria's garage more often, even when the price or location wasn't the best.

But Gloria also put the full force of digital tools to work for her. Whereas Bob was content to have his garage pop up on a Google search, Gloria wanted to have a more direct one-to-one connection with her customers. So she instituted a loyalty program, which customers could sign up for from a link printed on their parking ticket. Gloria also made sure to advertise the rewards program in the garage, showcasing the savings and the benefits. During peak times of the day or season, Gloria would allow members to reserve a spot in her garage. She also added other perks, such as car washes and tire checks. Gloria experimented constantly—different savings options, different rewards—utilizing social media. She encouraged her team members to present their own ideas to her—where could they reduce that gap between customer and company? How could they better serve their clients?

Her team knew Gloria's goal when they came to work every day. On their office walls was a sign that read: "A smile when they leave." *That* was the emotional response Gloria wanted to elicit from her customers—a sense of contentment that they chose the *right* parking garage, not just the one that was cheapest or most convenient. A parking garage that saw its basic purpose as serving people, not parking cars.

NEVER SAW IT COMING

As the months went by, Bob's amusement at the upstart across the street turned to anger. His monthly numbers kept falling and Bob couldn't understand why. His prices were lower than Gloria's! All else being equal, he should be crushing the new kid on the block. And yet he was losing. So Bob went back to what he knew: he cut costs even more. He laid off more employees. He skimped on cleaning and maintenance. He brought his rates down to the absolute bare minimum—and it just kept getting worse.

After decades in business, Bob finally decided that it was time to close his doors. He blamed bad luck and fickle customer demand. What more could he have done? His father managed a successful parking garage on a simple credo: "Beat 'em on price." Bob had done that. But he hadn't beaten Gloria. The writing was on the wall and it was time for Bob to sell. He did, however, have one last laugh when he saw who had made him the best offer.

It was Gloria.

CHAPTER 4

THE WORLD AS IT IS

I t's easy to be tough on Bob, our hapless parking-garage owner from the previous chapter. He's the fall guy to Gloria's business heroine. He does everything wrong so that Gloria can do everything right. But while Bob might be a bit of a caricature, it's not just his tone-deaf actions that are important; it's his *reasoning* behind them.

Why did Bob do the things he did? Because that's what his father did—and it worked pretty well back then. That's the point. *Back then*, a parking-garage owner only needed to compete on location and price. *Back then*, a parking-garage owner only needed a skeletal crew to manage the day-to-day operations. *Back then*, a parking-garage owner didn't expect much from his employees, who didn't feel like they needed to offer much. *Back then*, customers didn't expect anything more than an affordable, relatively clean place to park their car.

All these assumptions were true *back then, in the world that was.* Which means Bob was absolutely right; he was only off by twenty years.

Gloria's great insight is that we don't live in that world anymore. The economy has never been static, and it's old news that businesses, to remain competitive, need to stay up to date on the latest trends and technologies. The clearest example of this is that a software company like Google now makes self-driving cars, while a car company like Chrysler makes software. But you don't need me to tell you that.

What I am saying, however, is that the degree to which the world has changed, and continues to change, doesn't just affect what businesses create and provide. It also affects the people who produce *and* buy those products and services. It wasn't enough for Gloria to install automated ticket machines. A leader who was just trying to stay ahead of the tech curve would think that's sufficient (as Bob did). What Gloria saw was that her customers expected more than a smooth check-in and check-out experience. This led her to see value and a competitive edge in her own workforce, which, in turn, led her to develop a team that was more than just a group of parking attendants.

The rate and degree of change in today's world has impacted employees and consumers at a level most business leaders simply don't appreciate or understand. It's a behavioral change that, for reasons we'll see in a moment, has transformed not only how businesses operate, but how leaders lead. In other words, the greatest change that we've seen in the last twenty years is not technology; it's followers—employees and consumers.

Until now, we've discussed intentional leadership as the marriage of clarity with intentionality—of knowing where you want to go and how you want to get there through consistent action. In the last chapter, we saw how Gloria, as an intentional leader, took consistent action to achieve her goals, and perhaps her choices seemed rather specific to her particular circumstances. You, in another industry, might take different actions.

But there was an underlying reason for each action Gloria took. And while the specifics vary from business to business, the reasons shouldn't. Those reasons don't change because they are created by the forces that the world as it is has unleashed. To understand the reasons behind Gloria's actions, we first must understand those forces.

THE EXPLOSION OF EXPERIENCES

We first need to look at the world of the consumer. Much of the following story will be familiar, but it's the ramifications that should be enlightening.

Today's consumer has more power at his fingertips than the greatest kings of old. From a single device that fits into our pocket, we can talk to someone on the other side of the world, we can order dinner, we can conduct business and banking, and we can lose ourselves in a television show or game. The digital revolution has turned every person into a hub of information that dwarfs the most powerful computers of just a generation ago.

The smartphone is the easiest way to visualize this consumer transformation, but of course the digital revolution doesn't end with the smartphone. The rise of connected gadgets—otherwise known as the "internet of things"—has turned everyday household appliances into little nodes of data collection and transfer. Even our cars, as indicated above, are better understood these days as computers with motors attached rather than the other way around. We're only a few years away from entirely eliminating the role of the human driver.

The purpose of all this data collection isn't simply to make our user experience quicker or more efficient. It's to help us make decisions. The great promise of Big Data is in its predictive ability—in analyzing these zettabytes of data to find behavioral trends in *us*. To know what we want before we know we want it. That way, the app, gadget, or car can help us make a better decision, whether it's what to buy, where to go, or what to do. Alexa, Siri, and the other digital assistants flooding the market are more than simple voice-activated keyboards; they use our behavior to anticipate our actions and wants.

The basic point of all this is to get consumers to buy more stuff: to see that product pop up on your screen that you never knew existed or to be told that your printer is out of ink—and the printer goes ahead and just buys more. But there's another element at play, one that is mostly brand-new to the world as it is. It starts with the *feeling* consumers get when all these digital tools work in our favor. It's the little jolt of happiness that comes when Amazon's package shows up at the door the next day; it's the surprise when our online reservation is returned with an actual call from the restaurant confirming our reservation; it's the satisfaction of seeing Netflix suggest a new show to binge-watch.

Of course, consumers have been getting happy (or upset) with their purchases for millennia. Nothing too new about that. Rather, it's the feeling of *success*—that we've been able to accomplish something that we otherwise wouldn't have accomplished, that this company with which we interact empowered us to get more, do more, and be more.

The customer experience of success, whether it's to be happier, healthier, or more profitable: *that* is what companies are now competing on—and will be in the future. Look at it as if the consumer is a business unto himself and that companies are the vendors with whom he interacts daily. Businesses work with vendors so that they can be more successful.

And it's the same now with consumers—businesses and companies are now vendors to the powerful hub of information that is the consumer.

The problem for businesses is that now this expectation of success is part of consumer demand. We don't just want to buy a cheap, tasty pizza and have it delivered quickly; we want to feel *good* about how quickly we were able to buy that cheap, tasty pizza and have it delivered. We don't just want to park our cars in a parking garage; we want to feel good about choosing *this particular* parking garage over the rest.

With the hordes of alternatives on the market for every conceivable consumer wish, success is the greatest differentiator in today's world. To deliver an experience that leaves your customer with a swell of satisfaction because *she chose your company* is where businesses compete. Technology and the ever-changing state of the economy have not simply changed what consumers want; they've changed what consumers expect and, in turn, how they behave.

A WORKDAY OF MEANING

Just as they've had to deal with consumer behavior and expectations, businesses have had to grapple with a changing workforce. Many critics love to bemoan the scourge of the millennials and their absurd and ridiculous expectations on the job. The usual litany goes something like this: they don't want to pay their dues, they demand too much coddling, and they expect too much reward. While I don't think these are accurate critiques of an entire generation, addressing that is beyond the scope of this book. But what is often missed in the lamentations about the millennials is that the same forces that have changed the consumer have changed them as employees—and it's not all for the worse.

It's understandable that a generation raised in a society where want and deprivation are foreign concepts grew up expecting more than a paycheck at the end of the day. From the time they could walk they have been connected to the entire world, with the power to put their mark on it—through websites, social media, and video—in a way previous generations never knew. And when you're not scraping by for a living (although there are worrying statistics of how many thirty-somethings live with their parents), then you aim for more than an "attaboy" on the job.

A recent study found that 90 percent of business school students said they would be willing to sacrifice some percentage of their salary to work for a responsible employer. Fourteen percent even said they'd be willing to give up 40 percent of their salary to do so. We can laugh at a bunch of overprivileged MBA students haggling over money they haven't made yet, but we should take these statistics to heart. In fact, the article reporting the study noted that similar studies conducted in the 1980s and 1990s found that "business students were more unethical and more corruptible" than their counterparts today.[1]

Corporate responsibility, ethical behavior, philanthropic initiatives—these are the terms students in the study used to describe their perfect employer. It all boils down to one overarching idea: the rising generation wants *meaning* from their workdays. Technology and the changing economy have transformed the expectations and concerns from previous generations from the material to the ethical. The cynics cry that it's all a bunch of nonsense from entitled kids. But just as consumers have redefined their expectations for businesses, so have younger workers redefined their expectations for employers. There's no reason to put a value judgment on it. It's the new reality, and the intentional leader accepts it as opposed to shaking his fist at "those darn kids."

Moreover, the expectation of the employees bears greatly on the expectations of the consumers. To deliver an experience of success to a customer, a business needs to look beyond the straight calculus of value and price. It needs to understand that consumers are looking for something that they can't manufacture in a factory but can certainly create in their interactions. Those enhancing, refining, and augmenting those interactions between consumer and company are the employees. Whether it's the front-facing customer service reps or the programmers behind the scenes, they must be committed to creating a better, more successful experience.

The intentional leader doesn't look at the expectations of the rising generation and say, "We need to change that mentality!" He looks at them and says, "How can I make that mentality work for me?" Let's return to Gloria, who wanted to hire a workforce who believed they were responsible for more than just parking cars. To generate the customer experience she wanted, Gloria needed employees who worked for more than simply a paycheck. She wanted employees who worked *for the customer.*

As a leader, you might miss a simpler (but not necessarily better) era when the only thing employees wanted was a decent paycheck. But as an intentional leader, you must learn how to use employee expectations to your advantage. How do you leverage their desire for more meaning out of their workday to produce a better product? How do you entice an employee to go the extra mile for a customer?

By giving them what they want: inspiration. If employees want to believe they are working for something larger than money, then the intentional leader must find—or create—the greater meaning.

THE CULTURE CRISIS

The final force at work in today's economy is what's going on in the organization itself. Again, the changing expectations of the workforce have changed the organization, just as the changing expectations of the consumer have changed the workforce. For the organization, we're talking about perhaps the biggest buzzword in corporate literature today: culture.

In the pages ahead, I'll simplify what culture is, and how to create and maintain it. But right now, we're going to look at why culture has become such a hot-button topic. The question is: Why did the old ways of corporate life suddenly become oppressive and unfulfilling for employees? The first part of the answer has to do with the changing workforce, referenced above. But the second, deeper part of the answer goes back to the world as it is and the radical transformation the economy has experienced.

It's no secret that business moves faster today. The speed with which companies *work* far surpasses anything from the world that was. As a function of technology, this acceleration affects both large and small businesses alike. A food stand on the corner might not have had the corporate hierarchy that defined such behemoths of old like IBM or Pan Am, but its owner still ran the business at a pace commensurate with the speed of the economy. Information was slower, deliveries took longer, manufacturing was more ponderous, and customers were more patient.

The relative slowness of the economy allowed—and encouraged—an organization to have a culture that matched the way it did business: slow, steady, and without great upheavals. Where today a leader's forecast might be obsolete in a matter of months, yesterday's leaders could plan for ten, fifteen, twenty years ahead. Where yesterday it might take weeks to organize an all-company meeting, today a leader can televise his remarks to the troops all over the world at a moment's notice.

When technology changed, so did the speed of business. And the speed affected not only how companies were able to serve their customers but also how they treated their employees—or didn't treat them. Companies that adopted policies that allowed for swift, efficient changes were better suited for today's world. Companies that empowered their employees to make changes themselves could confront the new business climate better than those that adhered to a strict, cold hierarchy.

As with customers and with employees, technology changed organizational behavior. Old habits and ways of doing business suddenly became obsolete—even if those in charge didn't realize it. If you want your employees to take ownership of their jobs and make decisions that match the speed of business, then you can't treat them like cogs in a wheel. If employees demand more meaning from their employer than a paycheck, then companies need to rethink the way they do business.

It's no surprise why the start-ups that turned into today's tech giants pioneered our society's newfound emphasis on creating a corporate culture that *matched* purpose with meaning. Their swift and amazing rise to dominance forced them to move away from the "garage" feel of the start-up. They quickly became large corporations, even as so many tried to hang on to the start-up mentality. A lot of them failed, but at least the link was established: a company's culture was more than how it did business. It was how it stayed nimble and efficient in an ever-changing economic climate.

The power that a single worker could wield is astronomically higher than anything businesses a generation ago could have imagined. And with greater power comes greater importance. Companies could no longer afford to look at "the workforce"; they had to start looking at employees as individuals. And individuals are moved by a lot more than monetary incentives. We can take this appreciation for the individual a step further. Employees have become aware of their importance and thus a term was born that has come to plague the economy at large: employee disengagement.

THE THREE IMPERATIVE CHANGES

When Gloria set out to create a company that focused on customer service, she understood the power of these three forces. She knew that her consistent action toward reaching her destination depended on her ability to harness these three forces into a coherent whole. First, she set out to create a corporate culture that emphasized customer satisfaction and employee engagement, then she wanted to motivate and inspire her employees to believe that they were part of something larger than a parking garage, and finally, she put her company's efforts toward eliciting a positive emotional response from her customers.

Inspiration, culture, and emotion—these are the three imperatives of the intentional leader. They are the focus of that consistent action that a leader must take to reach her destination. While every company will approach these three imperatives differently, they are the backbone of a successful organization. More, they are the essential elements of intentional leadership.

CHAPTER 5

HIGH POINT UNIVERSITY

How does a sleepy, stagnant college that few have heard of increase undergraduate enrollment 259 percent in twelve years?[1] Furthermore, what enables a school to expand the size of the campus from 91 acres to nearly 500 acres,[2] while attaining a 97 percent career and graduate-school placement rate?[3]

The short answer is intentional leadership. The longer version is that an intentional leader revolutionized the academic institution of High Point University with powerful and practical business principles that often received sharp criticism but ultimately proved to be wildly successful. It turns out that academia, like most professions and industries, values the status quo.

Originally founded as High Point College in 1924, this private liberal arts university in North Carolina has grown from 22 to 112 buildings in the past twelve years. There are now 1,900 positions—1,600 of them full-time—and they hire twelve to twenty more people each month. These employees act to support the students drawn in from nearly fifty countries and all fifty states. HPU's incoming class of 2023 will be larger than the entire student body was in 2005 and will have access to fifty majors and fifty-seven minors.

And here is the brand promise that drives it all: *At High Point University, every student receives an extraordinary education in an inspiring environment with caring people.*

Nido R. Qubein, PhD, an alumnus of High Point University, became the seventh president of this ninety-five-year-old institution in 2005. After a successful career in publishing, consulting, speaking, and

business, he was approached by the board to help resurrect the institution. Always open to new challenges, he seized the opportunity to lead a
university whose facilities were a bit long in the tooth and that lacked any
signs of innovating in the future.

Similar to what we learn from physics, a system at rest stays at rest,
and Qubein had to challenge the existing mind-set and behavior of
faculty and staff who were mired in outdated educational methods.
He made it a goal to provide life preparation for students to take their
place in society after graduation. As Qubein often shares with faculty
and staff: "Our job is to prepare students for the world that will be, not
as it is, not as it was."

So how did he meet the challenge of changing the staid academic culture
to one that is unique and innovative today? Again, the short answer is hard
work. But the longer answer is hard work informed by visionary strategy.

When Qubein took the leadership role, the university's culture wasn't
defined. It just existed, the culmination of former leadership—the good,
the bad, and everything in between.

The first item of business was to change the existing mind-set. People
sometimes forget that while colleges and universities do not function
quite like most businesses, they still have clients. Students, either by loans
or scholarship, exchange money for a service—and they can certainly
choose to get this service from a different establishment.

This was part of the problem at the college. Because the various departments were not focusing on the customer, the institution was not optimized
for their use. Everything operated as its own unit. Groups didn't connect.
There was no sense of a larger purpose or united goal. Qubein started
having meetings with everyone together at one time, which may not seem
so extraordinary today but was certainly a change for the school.

Dr. Qubein began discussing the importance of branding with the
staff—a conversation that has not stopped. During meetings to this day,
he brings up the brand promise they established, reiterating vital points
to keep the ideas fresh. He incessantly educates those around him on the
responsibility of being a leader, advising with time-tested principles and
customer-focused perspectives, so the leadership at HPU can eventually
function on its own.

"He passes along what he knows," said Roger Clodfelter, senior
vice president for communication. "So HPU will thrive even when

Dr. Qubein isn't leading the place." If there is a consistent theme about leaders, it is that they are incessant in talking about the important things. This leader does not leave the future to chance; he has made decisions clearly leading toward the ideal future.

At HPU, literally everyone is empowered to make suggestions on how to improve *any* area of the organization, not just their own area. True to this, Qubein likes to be involved in all aspects of the university, no matter how small. As he described it:

> My first month in office, I would give out my email address freely to any student who wanted it. And they would use it! Students began emailing me—about a plumbing problem, a question about career options, or just to say how much they enjoyed a particular professor. I still provide my email address today so I can continue communicating with our students.
>
> The staff and faculty thought I was crazy to do this. "How will you ever get anything done if you have students constantly emailing you?" they said. My response was: "How can I get anything meaningful done if I *don't* have students connecting with me?"

The customer had become the priority: students, prospective students, and their parents are priority number one, although many other constituents like faculty, alumni, and donors are greatly valued and cared for. Roger Clodfelter, who was already at HPU when the transformation began and has borne witness to all the positive changes, credited the president's habit of hands-on involvement.

"The principle of inspecting what you expect is powerful," he explained. "So, Dr. Qubein spends a lot of time walking around campus. He's in front of students all the time, highly visible, and very much loved." Out of sight is out of mind, so it only follows that the opposite would hold true.

This also keeps the staff accountable. The reality of Qubein's engaged enthusiasm is that he has a high standard for others as well as for himself, and he's present to see if they are following through. Clodfelter continued: "It is hard to be at rest when the CEO could walk by at any moment, shoot you an email, or ask you a question."

LEADERSHIP BY BEING ENGAGED

When he became president, Qubein began using the power of observation to make important improvements. For example, he studied the flow of students between classes.

"Walking in single file," he noted. "*Not good*. The sidewalks were too narrow. I didn't want our students walking single file, lost in their own thoughts. I wanted them walking side by side, talking to each other. These sidewalks needed to be ten feet wide."

He made a mental note: *Change the sidewalks*.

What President Qubein does isn't just basic MBWA *(management by wandering around*, as coined by Tom Peters).[4] He sees it as a primary way to inspire: "I just get in front of our team. I walk around and pat people on the back, shake hands, share a laugh. It's not complicated." The connection with students is one of the most important aspects of his day.

"People don't care how much you know until they know how much you care," he elaborated. "I make time for moments of joy each day, and the time I spend in the café talking to students and staff members makes me feel good. Students take selfies with me. If a student is on their phone talking to Mom or Dad, I grab it and talk to their parents. I'm present."

As much as the president observes others, he expects to be observed in return. One might even say that he relies on it and models the behavior that he hopes the students will emulate.

"Whether you teach or not, students are watching all of us, so they learn from us. It is important how we act, dress, and talk," Clodfelter said. Done with intention, observed actions can become learned behaviors. Some of these behaviors are specifically geared toward the success of the students individually, but Hight Point University also hopes that these behaviors will improve their general quality of life.

For instance, environment is critical at HPU. When inspiration is part of the brand promise, you've got to deliver. This is physically done through gushing fountains, thirty-six sculptures of famous people, onsite concerts, and a plethora of free perks for students. Beautiful and clean areas are a necessary part of the aesthetic.

With a campus that has become so large and holds so many people, you might expect a certain amount of trash. You'd be wrong, however; they haven't even needed to post the obligatory "Don't Litter" signs.

Why? Clodfelter explained that "students know that just doesn't happen here. They also hold the door for visitors and each other." Thus, the culture is self-perpetuating; students see others improving the condition of life on their campus and then strive to contribute to it.

INSPIRATION BY EXAMPLE

High Point University has attracted expert faculty from places like Duke, Harvard, Stanford, Cornell, Johns Hopkins, and many other impressive institutions. Despite this progress, the school decided they could do even more.

By now, you know that Qubein is not your typical college president. His background in business sets him apart, and he is the recipient of many awards and honors. Those include the Cavett Award (known as the Oscar of professional speaking) from the National Speakers Association and the Ellis Island Medal of Honor, which has been bestowed on notable persons such as former president Bill Clinton and former British prime minister Tony Blair. Qubein is also the recipient of the Horatio Alger Award, which honors the achievements of outstanding Americans who have succeeded in spite of adversity and emphasized the importance of higher education; its recipients include Oprah Winfrey and Colin Powell.

Qubein accomplished much in business and served as a consultant to major corporations before becoming HPU president. So, in addition to HPU students having access to an impressive faculty, Qubein understands how important it is for students to learn from a variety of real-world practitioners and innovative thought leaders. In order to provide the best service to their students, HPU has also attracted global leaders and industry giants to mentor students as part of a unique "in residence" program. Examples include:

> **Steve Wozniak:** Apple cofounder and HPU Innovator in Residence

> **Marc Randolph:** Netflix cofounder and HPU Entrepreneur in Residence

> **Joe Michaels:** Twenty-two-year veteran director of NBC's *Today* show and HPU Broadcaster in Residence

Betty Liu: Bloomberg Television anchor, cofounder of Radiate, Inc., and HPU Media Entrepreneur in Residence

Cynt Marshall: Dallas Mavericks CEO and HPU Sports Executive in Residence

Bob Ryan: *Boston Globe* sports reporter and HPU Sports Reporter in Residence

Working closely with people who have already shown success in their fields provides students with mentors who have real-world experience and advice. It's one more thing pushing forward to the world that will be, both when those students graduate and when they start to change it themselves.

In addition to these in-residence faculty who regularly work with HPU students, HPU also attracts impressive speakers, leaders, academics, and scientists to major events such as the annual commencement ceremony. Past HPU commencement speakers include Condoleezza Rice, sixty-sixth secretary of state; Colin Powell, former secretary of state, chairman of the Joint Chiefs of Staff, and national security adviser; Josh Groban, internationally acclaimed singer, songwriter, and actor; former First Lady Laura Bush; NASA astronaut Buzz Aldrin; Muhtar Kent, former CEO of the Coca-Cola Company; and Dr. Michio Kaku, theoretical physicist and cofounder of string field theory.

And, to top off the list of accomplished faces on campus, HPU recently hired National Collegiate Athletic Association (NCAA) championship–winning coach Orlando "Tubby" Smith to lead its men's basketball team. Smith is an HPU alumnus who led Kentucky to the 1998 NCAA championship and has made a total of eighteen NCAA tournament appearances. Smith recently scored his six-hundredth career win at HPU.

DON'T LET CRITICS DRIVE YOUR BUS

Though the success of Qubein's changes is apparent now, they were not always so popular when he introduced them. Early on, HPU instituted valet parking.

Valet parking at a university for students? Are you kidding me? The dissenters fumed about spoiling the rich kids who went there. But Qubein didn't see it that way.

"There is a higher purpose for everything we do," he explained. "If your son or daughter has to park off campus and walk through two blocks of a poorly lit neighborhood late at night, you're going to worry. The valet parking was a solution to provide higher security and safety." Securing the confidence of parents, as well as the safety of the students, serves a dual purpose.

Today, HPU has no valet parking because lighting, security features, and security staff are ever present on a transformed campus.

And what about 1924 PRIME, where students get to experience global cuisine and practice professional etiquette as part of the meal plan? By the way, cell phones are banned from this restaurant. By now, I'm sure you know there is a reason for a learning lab such as this. Outside the restaurant, a mural quotes a *New York Times* article about interviewing potential employees. Often job interviews are held in a nice restaurant, and eating during a job interview is a frequent activity of movers and shakers.

Graduates need to know how to interact with executives, colleagues, and clients during a meal. The campus also has many boardroom settings for similar reasons: to adjust students to working in that environment. This is just another facet of preparing students for the real world.

Innovative educational initiatives like the President's Seminar on Life Skills, a required course for all entering freshmen, ensure students not only grow in specific academic areas of expertise but also develop competencies in communication, networking, coachability, fiscal literacy, and service. These are among the traits HPU refers to as "life skills," which employers have ranked in multiple national surveys as the skills most critical to succeed in the modern workplace. In fact, HPU conducted one of those national surveys in 2018. The survey of five hundred C-suite executives at companies with 5,000 to 25,000 employees found that employers would rather hire new college graduates with life skills as opposed to technical skills.[5]

Some critics may question some of the steps the president has taken, but he sees this as a burden of innovation. HPU students graduate with real-world skills that complement all they've learned, a definite contributor to the 97 percent placement rate.

Perhaps HPU's culture can be summed up in a quote from Roy Disney that's inscribed on the Kester International Promenade: "When your values are clear to you, making decisions becomes easier." High Point University has created its brand—realized what is important for the students and the school—and works to maintain it.

President Qubein has been crucial in accomplishing this. He sees two things as primary for a leader like himself to impact culture positively:

> First, they must model the behavior that is expected. I pick up trash, so everyone can pick up trash if they see it. Second, they must be a cheerleader for the culture. At HPU, we have monthly meetings with all staff where I spend time celebrating the best examples of our culture, reinforcing, rewarding, and, honestly, preaching! Our important language is present throughout our campus.

The recurring theme here is to lead by example. After all, if the president of the university is outworking everyone, how can anyone justify doing less?

EXPERIENCES THAT EVOKE POSITIVE EMOTIONS

Every university delivers an experience that differs in quality from institution to institution. The difference with High Point University is that the experience delivered is several levels higher than other schools. HPU may have had some catching up to do at first, but it didn't take long for Qubein to meet and then surpass the standards.

Upon taking the position of president, Qubein immediately led a $2 billion investment in academic programs and student life facilities, adding six new academic schools as well as two student centers, ten new residential communities, a new lacrosse and soccer stadium, a Division I athletics complex, and—currently under construction—a 4,500-seat basketball arena, conference center, and hotel. But again, the university didn't want to just catch up; High Point needed to become something altogether special, and that is what it did.

"HPU is an experience," Qubein shared, "that is distinctive with relevance. Our campus grounds are impressive. But that alone is not enough. We've invested $2 billion in our campus since 2005." The investment has permeated all aspects of the campus, including academics, technology, and experiential learning opportunities that teach students how to apply classroom content to the real world. And thanks to this transformation, robust programs have been established, including the Undergraduate Research and Creative Works Program, the Office of Fellowships and Awards, the Office of Career and Professional Development, the Service Learning Program, the Office of Global Education, the Professional Sales Center, the Belk Entrepreneurship Center, and many others.

It's why HPU is now a premier life school. The entire campus is designed to inform and inspire.

And the world has noticed. Since the transformation began, HPU has received national recognition. For example, HPU was included in the Princeton Review's Best Colleges list for the first time under Qubein's leadership, and every year since. In *U.S. News & World Report*, HPU was named number one regional college in the South for seven consecutive years and "Most Innovative" for four consecutive years. The university received a perfect overall score of 100 in the ranking.[6]

"I've never talked to a student or parent who said they enrolled because of a building," Qubein pointed out. "Our people, and I mean all our people—professors, security officers, campus enhancement team members, hospitality team members—all our people are recognized by our constituents for how we made them feel." Like all good services, HPU sets out to nurture emotions for its students, their parents, and its employees who interact with them; the interactions should be rewarding for all.

"We share testimonials that we receive from families," the president continued. "We've flown down parents and alumni to stand onstage in front of staff to tell them how important they were to their family." This way, employees get to see direct results of their efforts; it makes it easy to see how what you do really matters in the lives of others.

Qubein explained: "Humans are emotional people. There's really no other way to connect with people other than emotional[ly], not if you want a sustainable connection. For employees, we seek to create meetings that are experiences. Bands, visual elements, surprise gifts, and the like. If I can create the right atmospherics to inspire the team, they will inspire our clients." And when you reinforce those emotions, you perpetuate them; the students and their families benefit from properly inspired staff.

"People who visit don't want to leave," he said. "I've had parents tell me time and time again that it was a mistake making HPU their first college visit, because every other visit was a letdown compared to HPU." But it isn't just the experience. It is how students and parents feel about the experience; those strong emotions make up the foundation of a current and future connection with High Point University.

THE ART OF THE POSSIBLE

Not just any emotions will work for these connections, though. When asked about the emotions HPU strives to deliver, President Qubein answered, "I want everyone to believe in the art of the possible."

And just what is "the art of the possible?" Roger Clodfelter explained:

> When we talk about *the art of possible*, we use examples like building a $120 million health sciences building without a loan. In addition to modeling what is possible and raising aspirations, we like to use the university as an example of what a student can do in his or her own life. It becomes something that you can touch and see, a tangible example of what they can do if they work hard and apply what they've learned. You know that Farmers Insurance commercial? The one with the tagline "We know a thing or two because we've seen a thing or two"? At HPU we can say we know a thing or two because we've *done* a thing or two.

The school itself acts as a form of inspiration to the students. Not only has High Point University starred in its own transformation story of becoming a very prestigious school, but it took the struggles leading up to that point and made them part of the school's legend.

As you consider the HPU story, you can conclude that when you are in the transformation business, the proof isn't just in the students but in the campus, staff, operations, and even the nuances. Qubein put it this way:

> The worst feeling an employee or visitor can have is the feeling that they aren't important. If every person on your team believes they can have an impact, they can. And if they believe that, they will impact others in meaningful ways. At HPU, we talk a lot

about living a life of success and significance. Successful careers are important, but more so is leaving a legacy of significance. And that only comes from how you make other people feel.

If they had mostly good feelings, the experience will be positive. This is what every good business hopes and strives to create.

VALUING MORE

Beyond academic excellence, Hight Point University also focuses on values. President Qubein often explains that HPU is a God, family, and country school. While all backgrounds are welcome and celebrated on this inclusive campus, HPU appreciates and promotes the values of hard work, service, patriotism, private enterprise, joy, and generosity. To this effect, the school often hosts events to honor the people who exemplify these qualities.

Each year, HPU hosts one thousand local military veterans to express gratitude for their service to our nation. In December, HPU welcomes more than 30,000 visitors to campus for a two-night community Christmas event complete with a life-size nativity, falling snow, and Santa, who even offers a gift to each child. The entire event is complimentary.

And these are just a few examples of HPU's commitment to its community and its values. HPU students, faculty, and staff annually contribute 100,000 volunteer hours. [7] Qubein has raised $116 million private philanthropy dollars to revitalize the downtown of High Point, which was once a bustling furniture industry. Today, a downtown baseball stadium, events center, children's museum, hotel, and more are part of the core city's revitalization efforts thanks to his leadership, his support, and the transformation he's led at HPU.

Intentional leadership is not just being clear on what you stand for but courageous in how you implement your commitments. I toured the campus of High Point University extensively, and one of the beliefs they instill in staff is that "it might not be our fault, but it is our problem." Average service providers think that if they didn't cause a problem, then they aren't responsible for fixing it. People at HPU care about claiming responsibility for the solution—fixing the problem—rather than assigning blame.

High Point University is a values-based institution that believes each faculty and staff member has the power to enhance the lives of the students entrusted to their care. HPU's call to action is simple and profound: choose to be extraordinary! And their people live by it every day.

THOUGHTS FROM AN INTENTIONAL LEADER

In the president's seminar that Qubein teaches every spring, he has this discussion with the graduating seniors:

> When you go to interview for a position in your new career, you will not be judged on your strengths. Can you write a good letter? Express yourself with clarity and articulation? Dress presentably and carry yourself professionally in different situations? Good—*but so can everyone else*. These core competencies are crucial, but they will not propel you forward; they simply get you in the door. From that point on, what matters will be how you differentiate yourself.

Qubein knows that it is your decisions that bring you either success or failure, and he teaches his students this too. In the end, perhaps one of the most significant aspects of his service is knowing its boundaries. He cannot go out into the world for his students and solve their problems for them; all he can do is give them all the tools he possibly can—life skills, education, and the confidence to use them—and let them shine.

I asked Dr. Qubein what inspired him to lead. He said, "There are so many reasons: To whom much is given, much is required. I've been blessed by the help of others. And I understand that mentorship matters. It matters to me and our entire team here at HPU. It's a blessing to help others." This man clearly has a passion to serve his students, and it is reflected in every facet of the university.

If you get a chance to visit HPU someday, you'll be struck by the beauty of the campus, the friendliness of students and staff, the attention to detail, and the leading-edge learning opportunities. But you will see schools differently afterward, and ultimately something that Dr. Nido Qubein practices and proves: "To a business, *ordinary* is poison, *extraordinary* the antidote."

CHAPTER 6

THE CULTURE IMPERATIVE

YOUR ORGANIZATION IS A STRUCTURE, BUT CULTURE IS YOUR ENGINE

There is a higher purpose for everything we do.

—Dr. Nido Qubein

Ask a dozen CEOs what culture is and you'll get a dozen different answers. Ask a dozen CEOs how to create, change, and/or maintain culture and you'll get a dozen different answers. Few organizational topics, in my observation, are more discussed and written about—and less understood—than culture. It's no wonder that *Merriam-Webster* named *culture* the word of the year in 2014.[1]

The confusion is unfortunate because culture is the engine that drives *what gets done* and *how*. If an organization is the clock, then culture is all the tiny gears, widgets, and levers making the whole thing work. In chapter 4, we discussed why culture has become such a hot-button topic in today's world. In this chapter, we'll look at the *how*.

Culture has been one of the secret sauces of successful companies for years, even if the words used to explain it then were different: what we stand for, how we do business, what makes us different, what drives us, the way we do things, our definitive difference, and so on. These are various ways of talking about culture, although none of those phrases are comprehensive.

So the first thing we need to do is develop a *comprehensive* definition, remembering that this is how *I define* culture:

> Culture is what we think and believe, which then determines what we do and what we accomplish.

In other words, culture is the organizational DNA that influences what people think (intellectual) and feel (emotional, a critical component for the world as it is), which then determines what we do (behaviors) and what we accomplish (results):

> Intellectual + Emotional = Behaviors + Results

WHY CULTURE MATTERS

> *Performance more often comes down to a cultural challenge, rather than simply a technical one.*
> —Lara Hogan, senior engineering
> manager of performance, Etsy[2]

At a pan-European event, A.T. Kearney surveyed executives from one hundred firms and found that nearly 80 percent agree that culture matters greatly or is crucial to their organization's performance, but few monitor it (only 43 percent). Even fewer use cultural insights to shape strategy and operations (25 percent).[3]

So why does culture matter? Here are the six reasons:

1. *Culture is an immune system.* Wikipedia defines an immune system as "a host defense system comprising many biological structures and processes within an organism that protects against disease."[4] Culture is a corporate immune system that protects against variance, decline, or abandonment by identifying and combating threatening forces like toxic partners, disjointed processes, and bad decisions. This is why it's often so hard to "merge" corporate cultures in an acquisition:

competing cultures can each serve as competitive immune systems.

2. *Your culture defines your brand from the inside out.* An inward-facing brand is what you think about yourself. An outward-facing brand—and the kind of great interest to marketers—is what others think of you. Too often the two are disjointed, creating at best an illusion and, at worst, a delusion. A strong culture helps you get your inner brand right and congruent with your brand in the marketplace.

3. *Culture is pervasive and impacts everything you do.* Done right, culture operates at both a conscious and subconscious level. Over time, through repetition and reinforcement, your brand informs and guides decisions and actions.

4. *Culture directs departments and teams.* Since culture transcends individual departments, teams can see how what they do supports and serves the greater good. Culture becomes the North Star. Departments are doing different jobs in different locations but are guided by the same shared source.

5. *Culture motivates (or demotivates).* Employees either embrace or resist culture. That's why it's so important to make sure that everyone from tenured employees to new hires embraces the same shared, healthy culture. Otherwise, people spend more time resisting than they do producing.

6. *Culture enables agility and innovation, while keeping the organization tethered to what matters most.* Bad culture is an anchor, but in the worst sense. It impedes progress and allows the company to be overtaken by outside forces. Good culture preserves the best of what a company aspires to do and be.

The inability of most organizations to create and nurture a good corporate culture has become one of the greatest business dilemmas of the world as it is. Part of the reason is that too many business leaders are trapped in old ways of thinking, of focusing more on the output of the organization—product, sales, profit—than the organization itself. After all, if you provide a clean, safe environment for your employees and pay them at a competitive rate, then you've done your job. You're not responsible for their happiness!

And this is one of the great misunderstandings about culture, one that so many business leaders actively oppose. The idea that you create a culture for the benefit of the employee—so that the employee is happier—is flawed. Employee happiness is a consequence of a good corporate culture, but it's not its purpose. Why? Because you could have the greatest corporate culture in the world, and it might not matter at all to one or more employees. Not every employee at High Point University is happy. Making people happy isn't the job of an intentional leader.

The job of an intentional leader is giving employees the tools—the philosophy, the training, the communication, and the incentives—to be *successful*. Where have we heard this before? That's right, when we talked about how consumers want companies to help them be more successful. An employee who leaves work each day might just be a miserable person. You can't help that. But does this miserable person feel like they were given what they needed to be successful? That's your job.

This essential misunderstanding between happiness and success is why so many leaders get culture wrong. Like Bob the parking-garage owner, they make decisions that *seem* to be the right ones but are based on incorrect reasoning. You can imagine that if one of Bob's employees told him that worker morale was low, Bob's response would be to put in a foosball table.

"Problem solved!" says Bob.

Problem not solved. Yet this "foosball solution" is the default response of far too many business leaders who don't understand the purpose of a good culture.

What would Gloria do? What would Dr. Qubein do? The very thing that Bob didn't: *talk* with their employees.

I recently attended a talk by Judith Glaser, an author and consultant who calls herself an "organizational anthropologist." She said something that I think hits the nail on the head: "Culture starts with conversations."

Why is morale low? Ask.

What do your employees need to be more successful? Ask.

What can you do as a leader to help improve the corporate culture? Ask!

Before we talk about anything else, we need to understand that, at its most fundamental level, a good culture starts when a leader recognizes the employee as an individual. Everything else flows from that basic premise.

Now we can get to the rest.

THE FIVE LEVERS OF CULTURE

There are five levers you can use to create, change, and/or maintain culture. Intentional leadership is about doing culture by design, not default. And as you'll read in the various organizational examples in this book, successful leaders aren't just clear on what they want their culture to be; they are also specific about what they do to create and maintain it.

Much has been written about creating culture, and much of what has been written is obtuse. You need tools, and the basic mechanics of culture, I've discovered, can be explained by the five levers. Levers help lift or move heavy loads, and creating or changing a culture can be quite a heavy undertaking. Your most powerful tools for shaping culture are found in these levers.

Lever 1: Philosophy

Imagine your organization's culture like a pyramid. At the bottom of the structure is the foundation, the sturdy, large bricks that will have to carry the weight of everything above. The irony is that this is the level that is the most esoteric: How do you do business? What is the philosophy of your organization? What does it believe and what does it strive to do—beyond making a profit?

What do you value? What is sacred and immutable? What matters most, not just in what you do, but also in how and why you do it?

Some organizations call this a mission statement. Others paste their values in list form on a plaque. The end result is less important than the process of discovering your organization's governing philosophy. Dr. Qubein's philosophy for High Point University was simple yet powerful: "At High Point University, every student receives an extraordinary education in an inspiring environment with caring people." That's its goal—that's what everyone in the organization is there to do.

But I can't say this any better than how air-cargo giant FedEx puts it on its website for all to see:

> To provide the level of service and quality necessary to become, and to remain, the leader in the air express cargo transportation industry, Federal Express has developed a unique relationship with its employees, based on a people-first corporate philosophy.
>
> Founder and CEO Frederick Smith determined to make employees an integral part of the decision-making process, due to his belief that "when people are placed first they will provide the highest possible service, and profits will follow." Resulting from this principle is the FedEx corporate philosophy: People-Service-Profit. These three corporate goals form the basis for all business decisions.[5]

The basis for all business decisions.

That's why philosophy is Lever 1. It is the beginning of the conversation with your organization, your executive team, and your employees. It sets forth the rules of the game, while at the same time explaining the conditions for victory. Here's where we want to go, but here's how we're going to get there.

The "but" is important. You can become the leader in air-express cargo in a number of ways, just like Uber became a leader in ride sharing and Enron became a leader in . . . well, whatever it was they sold. Being the leader, the best, the industry standard, is the goal, but the way you get there is your philosophy. And a philosophy acts like a guardrail—it keeps an organization and its people on a path that adheres to a set of core values. From the CEO down to the janitor, all members of the organization are expected to conduct business within these guardrails. Departure from the specified path might not necessarily mean termination, but it should be condemned and corrected.

And that's the second part about philosophy: enforcement. Enron was infamous for having its corporate values plastered all over its headquarters in Houston. Except there was no enforcement, especially at the top of the company.

The intentional leader not only helps devise these values, which often can be a reflection of her leadership style, but she also must embody them. Ronald Reagan was known for never removing his jacket while in the Oval Office out of respect for the presidency. Do you think any of his employees dared to remove their jackets and roll up their sleeves in a meeting? It's often simple actions like that that enforce a standard of behavior and conduct in an organization. If the leader does (or doesn't do) it, then the rest will follow.

Find your philosophy, then hold to it.

Lever 2: Hiring and Firing

Jessica Herrin, founder of Stella & Dot, said, "Shaping your culture is more than half done when you hire your team."

But not everyone thinks about their culture when hiring. Instead, they think about hiring the best person.

I've learned the hard way—as many managers have—that the term "best person" is an ambiguous phrase.

There have been times when I overemphasized the skill set an applicant brought to the job but never considered the cultural mind-set.

Put simply, the best leaders hire for culture, not just function. The reason that an organization's philosophy forms the base of the culture pyramid is because all other decisions flow from that, particularly the decisions to bring on (or remove) personnel. These days, the hiring practices of companies have become something of a competition over who has the most unconventional methods. Google is famous for throwing odd brainteasers at applicants, such as "How many golf balls can you fit in a bus?" Clearly, they want someone who is smart and can think on their feet.

One of the better interview tactics I've come across was from a friend of mine. The normal interview questions had ended and the hiring manager—in this case, the boss himself—started to shoot the breeze with the applicant. The topic turned to fantasy football, at which point the applicant's face lit up.

"Oh, you play?" asked the boss, setting the trap.

"I sure do," replied the applicant, walking heedlessly into danger. "I'm in four leagues right now."

Next!

If you know anything about fantasy football, then you know that there's a certain amount of management one must do to field a decent team every week. It's not an onerous amount of work—unless someone is managing four different teams. The boss could tell right away that this particular guy would spend some time at work managing his teams—the sheer number of leagues he was in plus his obvious exuberance for the game made that abundantly clear.

The point is that you hire people who are going to match your organizational philosophy. Whatever values you hold dear as a leader should be in evidence within your workforce. If you have your employees spend a certain number of hours a month doing philanthropic work, then you want to hire people who find fulfillment in those types of activities. If you value collaboration and a team that communicates well, then you don't hire the loner who wants to work from home—no matter how good at the job she might be.

A leader might be required to exhibit the values in front of his team, but his team is more likely to reflect those values if they hold them as well. Of course an applicant desperate for a job might well say anything to get one. One is reminded of the movie *Ghostbusters*, where Winston Zeddemore, looking to join the plucky group of supernatural exterminators, replies to a long list of ridiculous questions about whether he believes in such nonsense like the Loch Ness monster or the theory of Atlantis with: "If there's a steady paycheck in it, I'll believe anything you say!"

You need to be a little cleverer than that, like my friend was with his question about fantasy football. Again, it comes down to *talking* with each applicant, learning directly from them how they look at the world, how they view your company, and what role they think they can play. People will tell you who they are, if you let them.

Both Zappos and Amazon have a "pay to quit" program. On the surface that sounds ludicrous, but the reasoning is sound: the faster you help an employee decide they aren't a cultural fit, the faster you can find someone who is.

Of course, to hire and/or fire based on culture, you need to understand the important attributes of someone who will be predisposed to add to rather than detract from your culture. Letting team members interview a potential new hire to see if they think the applicant is a fit is an old idea, but it's still helpful for hiring for culture.

Lever 3: Education and Training

Education changes what people think, and training changes their ability to do. Both are about learning and are important in shaping culture, but I'd put my biggest bet on education.

Hiring the right people who fit your culture doesn't help much if they don't understand how culture impacts their work. How overtly do you talk about culture in new employee orientation and training? Most companies don't spend any time on it because they aren't clear on what they want their culture to be. So they can't very well teach it.

James Hill, guest and team member experience director at Cumberland Farms, said: "The leader has to explain what culture is, why culture is important, how to achieve the desired culture, [to] be honest with the team regarding bumps and bruises that will need to be absorbed along the way of creating [the] desired culture, and, most importantly, hold himself and others accountable to deliver on it daily."

At Texas-based USAA, a diversified financial services group, all employees undergo a four-day cultural orientation. They are also asked to make a promise to provide extraordinary service to their customers, members of the military and their families.

Why is this noteworthy? Dr. Nido Qubein put it well: expectation without education equals frustration.

Education, as cited in all the case studies of this book, is always at the top of the list for getting people up to speed quickly. Not just on what they do but also why they do it—and how culture needs to direct their efforts.

Lever 4: Incentives and Reinforcements

In the world that was, salary and benefits were the twin pillars of any organization's incentive structure. The calculus was simple: people will work more if you give them more. A good salary and decent benefits still top the lists of what employees value most (things haven't changed *that* much), but they no longer suffice. A survey from Johns Hopkins University found that 95 percent of candidates believe that a company's culture is more important than compensation.[6]

This is eye-opening, if a bit vague. Each one of the candidates probably defines culture differently (although, I think that for many they mean the atmosphere or personality of their place of work), but the point is clear: for a company to attract and retain good people, compensation isn't enough. So what is enough?

Let's look at Gallup's "State of the American Workplace" survey. According to the results, when asked what attributes were most important in deciding whether to work for a company, respondents picked "the ability to do what they do best" as their number one response. The second most popular response was "greater work-life balance and better personal well-being."[7]

Again, employees are looking for a culture that allows them to succeed, not just on the job but also in other areas of their lives. A job that gives them satisfaction while there, but also gives them the ability to achieve success in their personal lives. Some cynics might read this and conclude that these candidates simply want to work fewer hours, but that's missing the point. Remember, the first response was entirely related to the job itself: the ability to do what they do best.

People want to find success on the job. They want to know their contributions make a difference and that they are valued. Rather than throwing money at the problem, the intentional leader looks for ways to *get out of the employee's way*. There are two words for this: autonomy and acknowledgment.

With autonomy, we can return to our discussion about the forces that have made culture such an important topic. Today's employees have the tools to be successful. They resent cultures in which they are watched like inmates in a prison. Probably one of the most egregious and invasive technologies developed in recent years is keystroke technology, which can track an employee's typing. Who would work for a company that has so little trust in its employees that it monitors their keystrokes?

Companies must be mindful of limiting employee procrastination, but that's also why they should be more mindful of their hiring policies in the first place. The growing desire of many employees to be able to work from home (or from anywhere) isn't so that they can binge-watch *The Walking Dead* (well, for most, anyway). It's so that they can manage the other parts of their lives that don't adhere to a simple nine-to-five formula—kids get sick, pipes spring leaks, and weather can be crummy. In the world that was, the manager would listen to these real excuses, shrug, and say: "Be at your desk." But in the world that is, the manager should say: "No problem, you can work from home."

Next is acknowledgment. Bonuses, raises, and greater benefits are all acknowledgments that an employee is doing good work, but they aren't the only ones and they're also not necessarily the most successful. People seek recognition and praise from their peers—this has been known for millennia. Psychiatric studies have shown that people will go to great lengths to avoid humiliation or embarrassment. Likewise, they will feel a swell of pride and happiness when they receive praise and encouragement. A gold watch for a job well done doesn't cut it anymore. A leader singling out an employee during the all-staff meeting, listing the great deed the employee did or the awesome sales figures she has accrued—now that's acknowledgment, and it's that type of praise that employees now crave.

Lever 5: Communication and Meetings

"You're on a need-to-know basis and right now you don't need to know."

This little military-inspired cliché was the *modus operandi* of the world that was. The thinking at the time was that employees only needed to be let in on matters that concerned them. Everything else was "above their pay grade."

Except no one likes to be playing the violin while the *Titanic* sinks. The idea that workers will be content to continue their work without any information regarding the true state of affairs is, like the *Titanic* itself, from a different era. Today's intentional leader strives for a culture of transparency within the organization, one that communicates where the ship is headed (and why the destination might be different than it was). This doesn't mean that all information should be made public—in a world of Twitter, that is just asking for trouble. Rather, it means that organizations should try to keep their employees informed as much as possible.

One of the greatest transformations that has affected the business world is the shift from a top-down hierarchical structure to one where there is a team-like atmosphere. And at any moment in a game, every member of the team knows (or should know) the score. They know the game plan. They know how well the other team is playing. And they know what they need to do—how they can make a small but significant contribution—to achieve victory.

That's the mentality that governs the intentional leader—the members of the team must know the score. This requires transparency and a commitment to effective and constant communication between all levels of the organization. Moreover, as we saw with Gloria and her interaction with her employees, it requires that the leader is visible and available to the employees. We're back at the necessity of conversation—the one-to-one interaction between boss and worker, leader and follower.

There are innumerable ways of going about this. The one you decide on is entirely your choice. Just remember that your employees will figure out the score soon enough. They'd rather hear it from you.

A CULTURE OF SUCCESS

Culture stands as the first imperative of the intentional leader because it is the one that most affects all the others. When we discussed the forces that had transformed the world that was into the world that is, we started with the consumer experience. We've now flipped the script, because while the changing expectations of the consumer have affected the way a business operates, it's the way a business operates that can lead to a better consumer experience.

And it starts with building a culture that is designed around one idea: success. Success for you, success for employees, and success for the organization. Success starts with a grounding of philosophy and values and ends with a team working as one for a common end.

CHAPTER 7

ACUITY INSURANCE

U ntil my first visit to Acuity Insurance's corporate headquarters, I'd never seen a Ferris wheel featured at this kind of business—let alone inside the building.

Before I had quite wrapped my head around this and all the Ping-Pong tables outside the actuarial department, my host, Nicole, turned to me and asked, "Would you like to see the dungeon?" I asked her to explain the metaphor.

"It's not a metaphor," she said. "It is a real dungeon."

In a spare room in the basement of the building, there is a full-blown dungeon, complete with a skeleton on the torture rack, appropriately wearing an Acuity T-shirt. It is all great fun, and while that's not the only thing this highly successful insurer is about, it is certainly a factor in their success.

THE ATTRACTION

Acuity Insurance is the fifty-seventh largest insurer in the United States and generates more than $1.5 billion in revenue, achieving nearly four times the cash flow of the industry average with a profit margin eight percentage points higher than the industry average.

Based in Sheboygan, Wisconsin, they operate through 1,000 independent agencies and 1,200 employees. In 2017, the property and casualty insurer was named ninth in the top ten of *Fortune* magazine's "Best 100 Companies to Work For" list.[1]

My visit took place when I was invited to speak to their claims group. As my driver neared the headquarters, he pointed out a landmark in the distance that was impossible to miss. Acuity has built the largest flagpole in the United States, and while two other flagpoles in the world are higher (in United Arab Emirates and Mexico), Acuity's pole is 411 feet tall, supporting a 10,000-square-foot flag.

Considered the largest symbol of freedom, it attracts veterans and other visitors from all over the country, even if the visitors don't quite understand its purpose. In fact, there are several critical Yelp reviews written by visitors who expected to find an amusement park nearby and were confused by the lack of other attractions. Who knows if they would be pleased or disappointed to know that at least one such attraction is hidden in the building?

The Ferris wheel inside Acuity was designed by the same people who created the one for the Mall of America. Despite the difference in scenery, the ride gets plenty of action. Each year, 1,500 students ride the Ferris wheel and, according to CEO Ben Salzmann, "They all want to work here someday when they leave."

The evidence supports his claim. Only 4 percent of millennials see insurance as an attractive industry, but Acuity has been exceptionally creative in filling the growing pipeline for new employees. A prime example of this occurred during a job interview with a recent graduate. When asked why she wanted to work at Acuity, she reached into her purse and pulled out a T-shirt with the company's name printed on it. She'd won it at a spelling bee hosted by Acuity eighteen years earlier and had held on to it ever since.

"I've only ever wanted to work at Acuity," the candidate explained. From an early age, she had been inspired by the company, and it still motivated her as an adult. Though this was a special case, it really embodies the effect Acuity has on people.

It wasn't always like this, however.

When Salzmann arrived in the late nineties, the data showed that the company had a 28 percent turnover rate. The entire staff of Heritage Mutual Insurance, as it was then known, essentially quit every three years.

So what enabled Acuity to go from among the worst in class to one of the best companies to work for in America? To quote an overused but accurate phrase: this isn't business as usual, and Ben Salzmann is another example of a very intentional leader.

CLAIMS DONE RIGHT

"You were so nice to work with," a grateful Acuity customer told his claims representative admiringly. Her response: "Who did you think they'd send?"

What kind of experiences have you had when you've filed an insurance claim? Often, we experience insurance companies that meet the letter of the law and their contractual obligation, but the process of dealing with them incurs additional stress and triggers anxiety.

Many companies claim to do a better job, but Acuity delivers. They believe that they are rebuilding shattered lives, and so their claims team has the latitude to go above and beyond to get the job done. In some cases, this means forming a relationship that lasts beyond the completion of the case.

Skateboarder Billy Moyle was driving home from work when a truck turned in front of him. When he was extracted from the wreckage, he couldn't feel his legs.

Sandy Schneider had been in the workers' compensation claims department at Acuity for fifteen years and arranged a deep dive into his recovery. Acuity purchased him a bike for therapy, revamped his bathroom for access, and bought him a standing wheelchair.

Billy didn't want a van, so they found him a pickup truck specially equipped with all the controls on the steering wheel. These kinds of requests often required special approval, and Sandy advocated for his needs.

"Billy has always had such a great attitude," Sandy shared. "Working with him shows me I do make a difference in other people's lives."

Two years after the accident and with Billy's lawyers now out of the picture, Sandy started communicating with him even more.

"I couldn't even tell you how many hours I've spent on Billy's case," she explained. "The relationship between Billy and I, it's not just a claims rep and an injured worker. Billy's my friend." For Sandy, this is simply the natural progression, though she knows that many other companies don't feel the same way.

"I think relationships are very important, whether Acuity people have relationships with agents, insureds, or injured workers," she continued. "Relationships are what's important, and that's what sets Acuity apart from other providers." Billy now calls Sandy his "Wisconsin mom" and feels that she is invaluable.

"She makes my life so much better," he said. "No words could explain how much she's helped."

Acuity is playing a key role in restoring Billy's life and achieving his goal: to skateboard again one day. And that creates nothing but positive emotion for Billy. It should not surprise you to learn that he is not the only one to feel this way. Acuity has a 95 percent customer claims satisfaction rating.[2]

CLARITY AND INTENTION

While *acuity* and *clarity* aren't technically synonyms, the words have much in common. Acuity is a keenness of vision, perhaps an aspirational step up from clarity. This similarity is not an accident, as its leader, Ben Salzmann, is intentional about everything that happens at Acuity. The most important aspects of this, however, are operational excellence and their strategic plan.

"We are students of both the industry and society, and we always have a five-year major theme," he explained. They create a plan based on what they observe in the world, and then they follow it.

He described the process of educating employees: "We bring speakers in and have dinner with them so they get to understand our culture. Then they present to thirty strategic planning people and then later to 150 managers. We record the presentations so we can show them at our regular Lunch & Learn events open to all employees." Attendance isn't required, but those who do choose to come are provided a free lunch and are entered in a drawing for money prizes.

From these key expert presentations, they develop and draft twenty-five actionable insights and merge them into twenty-five strategic initiatives from the year before. One and only one employee is assigned to each initiative, but they meet regularly so they can ask for more money, more people, or to adjust the time frame if needed.

"We want each leader's face tied to the project," Salzmann explained. The average completion time of these initiatives is two years, and the employees present their initiatives to the executive team every quarter, which keeps them accountable.

THE ACUITY PIPELINE

Acuity has an eighteen-year pipeline of all the employees they need to hire. They start at kindergarten. How? They bring students in for events like chess tournaments, open to kindergarten through high school seniors. They serve food and provide gifts with Acuity logos. Since their parents bring them in, there is another touchpoint to demonstrate what it is like to work there. Some strategies even vary between locations.

As a farm kid myself, I was struck by Salzmann's approach to recruiting in rural Wisconsin: "The average farm family has five kids—one can run the farm and we will hire the other four. And they go to college but want to stay local after they graduate." By supporting groups like 4-H, by hosting events or sponsoring a calf, they can make sure that these kids hear Acuity's name early and realize that it is a future option for them.

Another example is hosting the Junior Achievement Business Challenge state competition, which allows them to be actively involved with students at many levels. It costs Acuity $40,000 to host, and while the event also has support from companies outside their area, those companies don't meet with the kids. Acuity, however, sees the advantage. They want as many potential employees as possible coming to meet inside the business so they can feed them, give them Acuity-branded gifts as keepsakes, and let them ride on the Ferris wheel.

INNOVATION IS AN OVERUSED WORD

Considering that many would call Acuity an innovative company, you may be surprised to learn that Salzmann is not a fan of the term. He prefers to spend time studying society, keeping up to date with other people's imaginations and aspirations.

"You can't innovate in a vacuum," he said. "If you take the best genius and give them a year, feed 'em the best food and lock 'em in a room—a year later they don't look so smart. Take the same person and let them talk and look around and interact, and they will come up with great innovations. Stimulus is critical." He tries to take in as many different views as possible.

"Read *USA Today* and *Wall Street Journal*," he advised. "Follow MSN, liberal and conservative perspectives, experts within and outside your field, and you might just reinvent the wheel."

THE CULTURE DIFFERENCE

A couple of years ago, forty Acuity employees spent a day filming and two weeks producing (all during working hours) a short YouTube video called "Acuity Zombie Apocalypse." In four minutes, it explains why people love their jobs at Acuity and showcases the enthusiasm and creativity they bring to their work. The tagline: "Acuity is a great place to work now . . . and after the zombie apocalypse!"[3]

There are lots of things to love, even if they didn't all make it into the video. When asked, some of the favorites that employees will mention are things like free food, from maple bacon to sushi on the way out the door at night to chocolate on their desks (and tickets to the chocolate fair); the amazing fitness center with a 27,000-square-foot facility (where you won't be surprised to work out with the CEO); the climbing wall; and the flexibility to resolve personal matters when the need arises.

That is not to mention the way that the company tries to support its employees' family connections. For instance, every year an employee's Girl Scout gets to sell 1,500 boxes of cookies. Once this gave the winner a total of 1,612.

In short, inspiration and culture are writ large and small in this company. People are excited about their jobs and happy to be there. The emotional connection is tangible: "When you like your job and your employer, you're happier working. You have proof that your employer values you as a person and not just [as] an employee."

To summarize it in one sentence: "The little things make Acuity such a great place to work."

CREATIVE CULTURE BUILDING

"We start building culture before or at birth," Salzmann likes to say. While amusing, it's also true: Acuity funded the only neonatal intensive care unit north of Milwaukee and south of Green Bay.

"So instead of Flight for Life that separates the mother and child, the child stays locally." This has resulted in some emotional encounters. While families are in the unit, they see a picture of Ann and Ben Salzmann waving at them, giving them a face to tie with the feeling of love and joy they experience being with their child. The Salzmanns rarely go into their local Target or grocery store without running into a parent or grandparent who thanks them for everything they have done.

Obviously, the facility does not exist in order to recruit babies, but it is representative of the compassion that draws people in. Once there, the culture of innovation and fun keeps them hooked.

It all begins with *fierce respect for the individual.* I've read many books and been to many conferences, and those five words are never used, yet the idea is vital. The NFL does a great job of this. Players are all about self-expression, appearance, rituals, and scoring celebrations, but if one lines up in the wrong spot or runs the wrong pattern, he'd be off the field in a play because the player's actions jeopardized the game.

Fierce respect for the individual is about freedom to do anything that doesn't negatively affect the game or performance. Corporate America continues to have numerous rules that don't impact results. Salzmann describes one such instance of a new employee who arrived barefoot to work. There was a bit of an uprising; people were concerned about hygiene. It turned out that her parents were missionaries and she hadn't worn shoes for years; now they made her extremely uncomfortable.

"But I decided, how can it hurt us?" said Salzmann. "Are the bottoms of shoes hygienic?" It may seem like a silly point, but it is demonstrative of the respect this company shows to its employees. Because the company values them and treats them well, the employees want the company to do well. And the company certainly does treat them well.

"We believe in events," the CEO said. It shows. Acuity has a twenty-nine-year-old female employee with a $2 million budget who plans events for employees to enjoy themselves, regardless of whether there is any special occasion to warrant it.

Every even Thursday of the month, they provide beer, wine, mixed drinks, and appetizers for employees and their families. The holiday party includes one of largest light shows you can imagine and employees each get a $700 gift basket that includes great traditional gifts *and* crazy gifts (mystery jelly beans that taste like earthworms or tangerines, for instance). In the past, they have rented roller skates for more than one thousand employees (three broke an arm) and let them glide around inside the building.

Each month, they provide something fun—"a trinket"—to take home. It might be flower bulbs to plant in the spring, fresh strawberries in the summer, or a basket of corn in the fall. Those rituals have become ingrained and always create a positive sense of anticipation.

However, don't presume that the generous gifts are because Acuity doesn't pay their employees fairly and well. They do fourteen different salary surveys to help determine where their compensation should be and provide a most generous health insurance option (so much so that if an employee is married to a teacher, they usually drop the teacher's plan for the superior Acuity plan). In addition, there is no match required for the 401(k) feature.

"We do everything we can plus a quart of strawberries," Salzmann explained. "Or giant Costco pumpkin pies. Nothing like coming into the building and smelling freshly baked pumpkin pies."

The results of culture by design at Acuity? Consistently excellent operations, rather than perfect.

"Execution is meaningless unless excellent," Salzmann elaborated. "But if you get tied up in being perfect, you'll never be great." Perfection isn't really achievable, and if you can't get past imperfection, you'll never move forward. Salzmann's method was to start advocating corporate decisions and getting in touch with the customers to see what is really important—how do customers define world-class service?

"We had to own our responsibilities," Salzmann said. "We know we can't do it to perfection, but always with excellence."

FAIL BY ACTION, NOT BY PASSIVE FEAR

Some training programs are essentially a boring hour with human resources, doing paperwork, maybe with an older employee assigned to "show you around." Not at Acuity. Salzmann described it in detail:

Every employee is given an iPad on their first day. We do a video on how to park, get through security, find the training room, where the restrooms are—everything they need to know. It is no insult to new hires; we do it to create a great experience and quickly help them understand not just the logistics but also our culture. Classroom instructors are in the video: "Hi, I'm Dave, and I'll be teaching . . ." We want to empower them, not hold their hands. We provide 2.5 months of classroom training. Then, for 1.5 months, they will watch someone experienced doing their job—an experiential mentorship. They can do this both from the classroom and in person. The workstations are designed to be conducive to this type of learning.

Above all, however, new employees learn Ben Salzmann's creed. While in Rome visiting Raphael's tomb at the Pantheon, Salzmann had an epiphany of sorts: he decided he'd rather fail by making mistakes than whimper and do nothing.

It became integral to his leadership philosophy as "Fail by action, not passive fear." When he shared this concept, it lit up feedback across the company. He decided that he needed to share it with Acuity's agents as well, so he established "Ben's Gossip Line," a direct connection to those 25,000 independent agents, and shared his new mantra. The response was powerful.

He got many replies, not just about business but also from listeners going through cancer and other challenges. They said it not only helped them make a sale but provided a good lesson to share at home with their kids. It was everything he could have hoped for and more; connecting with employees and business colleagues is as much about the personalization of a message as it is about the professionalism.

TOWN HALLS

Acuity has hired seven hundred new graduates in the last seven years, but none go far without learning to "fail by action, not by passive fear." The company encourages ideas and trying new methods and invites employees to share their thoughts. One avenue of doing this that Acuity is known for are its Town Halls, company-wide meetings held in their two-thousand-seat round theater with five Jumbotrons. The chairs are fully upholstered, and the longest distance to the center stage—from the back row, top balcony seats—is only sixty feet.

"Every quarter, we have the whole company stop work for two hours," Salzmann clarified. Voice mail messages say, "Sorry, but we are in a company-wide meeting; leave a message, and we will get right back to you." Officers individually go onstage and talk for just two minutes. A Q&A session follows, and employees can ask from the microphone or submit anonymously.

Acuity values the opinions of its employees and gives them opportunities to voice them. For another example, every holiday season the company invites six different charities to present their needs and values to the staff. Then the employees vote on how to distribute $500,000 among them. This is followed by entertainment, a little like *The Gong Show*. They've brought in top performers like the Blind Boys of Alabama, Kellie Pickler, and professional comedian and actor John McGivern.

AT THE LITERAL END OF THE DAY

When asked about the point of it all—the fun, the gifts, the training and development, the community outreach—Salzmann summarized by saying:

> You're walking out of [the] building at seven fifteen at night, you turn a corner and bump into an employee. Do you feel bad because you haven't ever connected with them or appreciated them? Or do you both have big grins because you have talked with them at breakfast, worked out at the gym at the same time, and know they love their job?

It is clear which outcome Salzmann expects, but there is another purpose for even further in the future: "We are all going to die someday, so it is all about how you face each day."

As for Acuity? The whole company sets out each day to inspire, appreciate, produce, and have a whole lot of fun. They may have a dungeon in the basement, but the Acuity staff certainly have the freedom to live fulfilling lives.

CHAPTER 8

THE INSPIRATION IMPERATIVE

FUEL MORE POWERFUL THAN MOTIVATION OR ENGAGEMENT

After I spoke to retailers at Park Meadows Mall, the largest in Colorado, I happened to meet Matt Allen, cofounder of a new company I'd been hearing good buzz about, NHiM Apparel. With his wife, Diane, the two started their company in 2014 with a clear motivation: "More than a brand. A movement. We create premium and original designs to reflect who you are and to share your faith. Proceeds help orphans and underprivileged families globally."

So what? Well, the first question is what does NHiM stand for? Answer: "*In Him* we live and move and have our being" (Acts 17:28).[1] An unabashedly Christian company serving Christian customers. The matter of religion is less important here than the clear *inspiration* that not only served as the bedrock upon which the company rests but also continues to power the company, and its founders and employees, forward.

Listening to Matt, I realized that here was a leader who wasn't interested in a brand, but rather a brand with purpose. He told me how their first batch of product—a dozen T-shirts—had created a buzz with friends and family. They wanted more Christian-themed apparel, which is how Matt and Diane soon realized that their brand had the power to become a movement. Their success grew so quickly that they went from one kiosk in Park Meadows Mall to a full store within twelve months. Plans are to open more locations throughout the United States.

All the while, NHiM uses its growing proceeds to help build orphanages and provide hope to children. They also help underprivileged families globally.

The idea of conscious capitalism isn't new. But the few who preach (or follow) the idea realize that it's as much for the success of the company as it is to help a particular cause. A conscious capitalist company that doesn't move product doesn't help anyone. The buried power of conscious capitalism is not in what it does for those outside the company; it's how it inspires those *inside* the company—to know that when they go to work every day to make more T-shirts that they are *a part of something bigger*.

When NHiM was founded, the leaders shared:

> We are a premium Christian clothing brand for men and women—promoting others to become everyday missionaries through casual conversations. These conversations can often happen over something as simple as a T-shirt or hat. We believe in being givers—giving back to build orphanages with the proceeds to give children a future filled with hope.

How do you inspire Christian believers into giving their all to produce clothing? By turning them into missionaries.

WHY INSPIRATION?

According to an IBM survey of 1,700 CEOs throughout sixty-four countries, the three most important leadership traits are:

1. the ability to focus intensely on customer needs;
2. the ability to collaborate with colleagues; and
3. *the ability to inspire.*[2]

Tying purpose to passion might seem easy for a Christian company. Yet recall how Gloria also inspired her employees at a parking garage—a company that clearly has no higher calling (in theory) than being a place where people put their cars. Gloria didn't need to donate any of her proceeds to a charity or support a cause. She certainly could have done that, but I assume that a parking garage runs on fairly tight margins. Her solution was to turn her employees into customer-service representatives first and foremost: their purpose was to serve the customers, to improve the experience of parking their car at Gloria's lot.

Likewise, the intentional leader doesn't have to look outside the company to find purpose. Nor must an intentional leader invent a purpose out of thin air. As an example, Gloria could have told her employees that she expected them to volunteer at a soup kitchen once a month. It's a nice gesture, but such a decision would do little to inspire her employees; they would likely see it as just an aggravation that has no connection to their day job.

Inspiration doesn't come from an outside force or artificial causes. It comes from the work itself. The Quality of Life @ Work study of twenty thousand employees in dozens of countries around the world found that workers have "four predictable core needs at work: physically, to rest and renew; emotionally, to feel cared for and valued; mentally, to be empowered to set boundaries and focus in an absorbed way; and spiritually, *to find a sense of meaning and purpose in their work*."[3]

Inspiration comes from doing the work, the day-to-day grind and monotony that so many of us loathe. As James Hill of Cumberland Farms said to me, "Inspiration is *creating an energy in oneself to achieve extraordinary things*."

DICHOTOMY IS DEAD

At some point in their career, almost everyone goes to a job they hate. There was a time when this was mostly accepted as a fact of life. It's called work for a reason, right? The dream for most wasn't money—although money certainly helps—it was to find a job that "didn't feel like work."

Some of us are lucky to find this in our careers. The rest of us have to work for a living, earning a paycheck, paying bills, and providing for our families. But in the world that is we have gravitated toward a different belief: If we can't be lucky enough to find our "dream job," then we would like to work for a company whose purpose goes beyond moving product and making money. The new economy has given companies the power to do more than simply sell. They can also give.

That dichotomy that our fathers and mothers had to accept—work at a job you hate so you can live a life you love—is over. Now we can work at a job that has meaning to live a life we love. It's the imperative of an intentional leader to give employees that meaning, that purpose, that sense that they are a part of something a bit bigger than just earning a paycheck.

In a word, the intentional leader provides inspiration.

The power of inspiration has already been measured. As reported in the *Harvard Business Review*, recent research shows that while engaged workers admirably perform at 144 percent of the rate of satisfied workers, inspired employees were 250 percent more productive than their satisfied counterparts.[4]

Fueling the surge of inspiration's importance are the much-maligned millennials. As the youngest generation in the workforce, this makes sense. They are a product of the new economy, entirely reared in the world as it is today. The rest of us remember the world as it was, and some of us still cling to the ideas and beliefs that powered that world. So it's no wonder that millennials put a higher emphasis on making meaning than other generations: 84 percent of millennials believe making a positive difference is more important than getting professional recognition.[5]

Some readers might quickly ask: Isn't inspiration just a fancy way to describe motivation or engagement? No. Motivation and engagement are task focused and lack the sustaining power of inspiration, which infuses purpose with motive. Rather than a temporary driver of success, it is the fuel that sustains it. At the 2018 World Economic Forum in Davos, Switzerland, Larry Fink, founder of $6.3 trillion asset manager Black-Rock, took center stage with what has become known as "Larry's Letter." In it he asserted a dramatic shift needed for better capitalism: "Without a sense of purpose, no company, either public or private, can achieve its full potential."[6] He went on to detail what happens to companies lacking purpose, which is a critical ingredient and driver of inspiration.

The dichotomy that our parents had to accept is dead. In its place has emerged a new reality: money doesn't provide passion, only purpose.

HOW INTENTIONAL LEADERS INSPIRE THEMSELVES

Matt and Diane Allen found their inspiration through their faith. They in turn inspired their employees (and customers) through faith. Gloria received inspiration from creating a parking experience that was not about cars, but people. The point is that to find the inspiration for your company, you first need to find it in yourself. I won't pretend that this is easy. Not everyone is in charge of a company that was founded on a set of inspiring bedrock principles. But that doesn't absolve the intentional leader of the responsibility to search deeply in herself to uncover those principles. They exist. And your job is to find where they exist in you so that you can bring them out in others.

Here are some tips on how to find that inspiration:

Solitude: The majority of a leader's day is filled with meetings and interactions. It is easy to get lost in the perpetual buzz of activity. Solitude never happens. You make time for it.

Calling: What you "have to do" pushes you. What you are "called to do" pulls you. Early in a leader's career he does what must be done. At some point leaders should transition into work that allows them to do what they want to do. Leaders become highly ineffective when they do only the things thrust upon them that are obligatory and don't focus on what they do well and what brings them enjoyment.

Circle: Few things impact a leader more than those we associate with. While we are acquaintances of many, we form our inner circle. Are you spending time with people simply for enjoyment or have you chosen to associate with those wiser than you who can challenge you to become better?

Wonder: Fuel your sense of it. When you've lost curiosity about your work—your profession or industry, your people or organization—you've lost the ability to be inspired by new ideas. Stephen Hawking said, "Be curious."[7] And I add to that, stay curious.

Humor: I have no quantitative research to back up what I'm about to say, but I have never met a truly inspirational leader who didn't have a well-developed sense of humor. To be able to see the absurdity in daily life, rather than feel overcome by it, is how we not only stay sane but also how we remember what's important. Research has been done and books have been written about the benefits of humor in communication and leadership. There is much information about this topic, and you might want to do a Google search for more specifics.

Thankfulness: The first act of every morning for me is to recall at least three good things that happened the day before. Even on the worst of days there are good things to recount. The challenge for most leaders isn't that they aren't blessed. It is that they aren't recognizing those blessings.

Contribution: The question of leadership isn't "How can I contribute?" The question is "How can I best contribute?" You will be most inspired (and inspiring) when you are making the biggest positive impact in your work.

Health: Why must leaders be reminded that without health, not much else works? We all can experience ill health without warning. But so much of basic well-being and the energy to lead are linked to foundational things like diet, exercise, and the avoidance of unhealthy behavior. Far too many leaders wait until their health is lacking to turn their attention to a healthy lifestyle. Besides, some of my best ideas come when I'm working up a sweat. Exercise is a great way to fuel your brain.

If all else fails, ask others what inspires them. What moves them to get out of bed each day? What fuels their desire to contribute, to produce, to create? The answers form the basic foundation of purpose. And to find your purpose is to find your inspiration. The intentional leader is a man or woman who has thought and continues to think deeply about their business, lessons learned, changes on the horizon, and opportunities to pursue in order to create informed understanding they can use to guide others.

TEN TOOLS FOR INSPIRATION

Of course, the goal is to find that inspiration that moves others, not only you. I need to be clear here. In the examples used thus far I have been able to show how companies have distilled inspiration down to a single purpose or phrase. But that gives a false impression that you must find a single purpose or phrase in order to inspire. This isn't the case—and hasn't been my experience. There is a thing called inspirational leadership, in which the leader is able to inspire without resorting to an idea or purpose. We find obvious examples of this type of leadership from military history, where the great generals of ages long gone were able to inspire their troops to superhuman feats and incredible displays of loyalty. In recent memory, we have also seen it in coaches, the greatest ones being those who are able, day in and day out, to get the most out of their players through inspiration. While a military leader might be able to point toward noble ends—the elimination of tyranny, the pursuit of liberty—a coach is left with little more than his players' competitive spirit. Yet that's enough for the best coaches to get just that tiny ounce of extra effort to win the day.

Inspiration doesn't have to be mysterious or complicated to create. What follows are tools used by the leaders I've worked with for over thirty years, as well as those profiled in this book:

1. **Connection:** All the leaders profiled in this book share the common characteristic of being highly visible and accessible to those they lead. No exceptions. Connection is more than visibility and accessibility. It requires the effort to spend time with those on your team without having an agenda. That opens the opportunity for deeper-level conversations, questions, and even mentoring. As Fritz Holding of Noble Oil told me: "To inspire others I tell hard truths when necessary to trigger positive action/reaction. Tell people about possible outcomes that can benefit them [and] the company, and ultimately improve the lives of others around them."

2. **Example:** If you are an inspired leader, your visibility will go far in inspiring others. Spouting bromides and acting like a bad game-show host isn't inspirational; it's cheesy. The key elements to a leader's example are:

   - courage—taking a stand and doing the right thing even when it is costly;
   - authenticity—being who you appear to be without pretense or arrogance;
   - commitment—investing your energy in your work, the success of the organization, and the success of others; and
   - behavior—what you spend your time doing, not just talking about.

3. **Integrity:** Integrity, as I define it, is the distance between your lips and your life. Disillusionment in our culture is high due to many high-profile leaders whose exposed behavior has proven them to be . . . well, jerks. Unfortunately, even the best leaders are suspect according to the cynics. Authenticity and integrity should never be in conflict.

4. **Understanding:** One thing that motivation and inspiration share is specificity. Different people are inspired by different things in different ways. According to Gallup research, the odds of employees being engaged are 73 percent when an organization's leadership focuses on the strengths of its employees versus 9 percent when they do not. Increasing engagement is about understanding the strengths of those you lead. It is also about understanding at an emotional level what matters to team members and how they feel. That is the understanding that comes from empathy.

5. **Purpose:** Pointlessness is wasteful, demoralizing, and the antithesis of inspiration. The purpose of the organization needs to be linked to every employee and every job. Linking the lower-level work to the higher-level purpose is one of the most powerful tools a leader has.

6. **Education:** Education has the ability to impact and shape lives. It can alert an employee to opportunity. It can draw

out things the employee didn't even know they knew. It can provide insights that might have been missed. And it enlarges their capacity to contribute and produce. All those benefits are inspirational.

7. **Challenge:** The best leaders challenge employees to become more than they are. They recognize legitimate potential and help employees pursue it. Leaders can inspire by raising the expectations they have of those they lead.

8. **Culture:** Inspiration means to be "in spirit." In the world of work, you are in spirit with your culture. A healthy culture inspires. A dysfunctional culture impairs even the most inspired employee.

9. **Appreciation:** Appreciation is more than a leadership tool; it is a fundamental human need. I've yet to meet anyone in my work who feels "overappreciated." However, appreciation needs to be more active than a simple thanks or expression of gratitude. It needs to demonstrate that the leadership values the employee, and it needs to be specific about why.

10. **Storytelling:** Good storytelling captures attention and educates as much as it entertains. From years of making a living as a professional speaker, I know that people don't remember points and facts—they remember the story. The story becomes the mental coat peg people then hang the ideas on. Inspiration comes from hearing inspiring stories that summarize and reinforce the purpose, culture, and important lessons of an organization.

You might use these tools to find that great purpose or idea embedded deep within your company. Or, more practically, you might use them to inspire your employees to work for you. That's just as effective as holding some higher purpose over their heads. Many of us have had that "great boss" who was able to get the most out of us. Why? Because we wanted to do our best for him or her. Of course, I can't be certain, but I can probably guess that that one great boss in your life used one of those tools above to push you to a stage of performance that didn't feel like work. It felt like you were making a difference.

SEVEN SHIFTS TO AN INSPIRED WORKPLACE

The result of a workforce that's inspired should be evident—greater performance means a better bottom line. Yet many of the true benefits of an inspired workforce go beyond money. They include:

1. **Pointless to purposeful:** Almost everything an employee does each day has a point to it, but far fewer things have a purpose. The point is the operational reason. Purpose is a higher-level resolve.

2. **Money to meaning:** It is far easier to make money doing a task, even something you hate, than it is to combine making money with making meaning. Yet making money becomes routine. The typical employee doesn't see her salary increase depending on the employee's daily performance—or the performance of the company. Raises or promotions occur gradually. Which is why money motivates performance, up to a point. But to make meaning—that is a tangible benefit that employees can see every day, assuming that the leader does a good job of showing them.

3. **Commanded to called (or pushed to pulled):** There are many reasons why the United States doesn't have a conscripted army anymore (or only during existential threats). It was learned that a volunteer army, made up of soldiers who wanted to be there, was more effective. To be coerced into doing something is to do the job poorly. You only do enough to finish the job. To be called to do something is to do the job until *you're satisfied* with the results. Not a boss. Not a shareholder—you. James Hill of Cumberland Farms pointed out:

   > When team members fail to deliver the desired result they pick themselves up on the field of battle, dust themselves off, and try even harder with different approaches to eventually deliver the desired results. As a leader you often have to sit back and watch team members struggle as they learn, although heartbreaking at times, and have to allow them that precious time to figure it out.

4. **Success to significance:** Success is about accomplishment and achievement. Significance is about fulfillment and contribution. Success is the end result; it's what happens when the work has been done. But what about when the work is *being done*? That's where significance comes in. Does the work itself, not the result, imbue the employee with a feeling of being helpful, of mattering?

5. **Endurance to enjoyment:** The old "nine-to-five." If ever a phrase captured the world that was, it was this. A worker *endured* the hours spent at work, waiting for the very minute, counting the seconds, until he could punch out. But an inspired workforce, one that is consumed with the purpose and the passion of their work, isn't bound by a time stamp, because the hours are enjoyable, not a grind.

6. **Experience to emotion:** How do I feel at the end of the day? Exhausted? Ready for a drink? Ready for bed? Or fulfilled and content? Being tired at the end of the day isn't a bad thing, but we all know the difference between good tired and bad tired. Bad tired means you're irritable, discontented, and impatient. You look for the reprieve in other things like television, your smartphone, or alcohol. Good tired is when you are relaxed, emotionally and spiritually. Having a positive experience at work is good. Feeling inspired and fulfilled because of the work experience is better.

7. **Routine to rewarding:** Day in and day out, the same nonsense. Routine is boring; routine saps our energy; routine ages us. Now, some work just needs to get done, and there's no way around that. But an inspired workforce is one where the day is spent on rewarding, not dull, activities, so that employees see the purpose behind what they've spent eight, nine, ten hours doing.

The point? Motivation always has and always will be important for the leader and her team. But today, inspiration is even more important. "The carrot and the stick" have been replaced by "the purpose and the mission."

Think about it: Would you rather create motivated work or inspired work? Your team will answer in the same way.

CHAPTER 9

SAVANNAH BANANAS

This is a story about the first baseball team named after a fruit and the man in a yellow tuxedo who leads them.

Baseball is a sport beloved in the United States and embraced internationally. The "great American pastime," as it is called, has inspired fans since it was invented in 1839. Who doesn't like baseball? Well, me. I'm not a big fan of the game. I will go when I get free tickets, to improve my suntan and drink some beer, but it can be very slow, tedious, and boring.

There are lots of people like me, even in Savannah, Georgia, who don't particularly like the game of baseball, but they love their Savannah Bananas summer collegiate league baseball team. That might seem confusing to you and understandably so—why would they want to pay money to attend a sports game they have little interest in? The answer may surprise you.

Baseball, I dare say, is really secondary to a crazy, fun-packed few hours that literally has something for everyone—from branded craft beer to shenanigans that would make P. T. Barnum (and maybe even the Las Vegas Strip) proud. Most significantly, it is led by an intentional and creative leader named Jesse Cole, the "fellow in yellow" himself.

FANS FIRST

Jesse's company, Fans First Entertainment, has owned and operated baseball teams throughout the last decade. The success speaks for itself, or rather, its fans do. The Savannah Bananas are the flagship team and have sold out every game for three straight seasons. The wait list for tickets is in the thousands for this season and will sell out every game as well.

They've been featured on MSNBC, CNN, and on ESPN multiple times. Their sensational antics keep the attention of the public, and it works in their favor: they've quickly won awards and accolades like Organization of the Year, Executives of the Year, and Sports Event of the Year. For a team in the lowest level of play, the team is well known. In 2015, Jesse bought the expansion franchise, and now Bananas merchandise is sold in all fifty states and numerous countries all over the world. The team even has its own branded beer.

Their great success is not an accident. It is built on a simple intention: to make baseball fun.

For the Savannah Bananas, this means putting fans first and entertaining always. That includes having dancing players, a breakdancing first-base coach, a thirty-piece Banana Pep Band, and a senior-citizen dance team called the Banana Nanas. There is even a TV series currently in production to document the team's crazy ride to success. I imagine there will be a great deal to cover, given the breadth of their activities.

The Savannah Bananas began playing in the Coastal Plain League in 2016. They've now had two seasons of sold-out college baseball, the lowest rung of minor league baseball. In 2017, they welcomed 108,498 fans, once again breaking the league's attendance record.[1] They also sold out all regular season games, with an average of 4,173 fans each night,[2] despite adding two hundred seats for the second season and another two hundred this year.

How does all this happen in an organization of 16 full-time, 150 to 200 part-time, and 10 full-time interning employees? The answer requires telling you a story, and it begins with the owner of the Bananas, Jesse Cole (whose Fans First business also bought the North Carolina Gastonia Grizzlies in 2014). And as Jesse himself says, it is all about the story.

THE STORY

Jesse and I first connected on his podcast, one of the most creative I've ever participated in. It quickly became apparent that this unique and passionate individual had surrounded himself with like-minded people and created an experience that customers clamored for.

Jesse Cole became the general manager of a college league baseball team at the age of twenty-three in Gastonia, North Carolina. Attendance was dismal at two hundred fans per game and the operation was losing over $100,000 a year. As he thought about the challenge he inherited, he had an epiphany: "I realized we can no longer be a baseball team. Baseball games are long, slow, and boring. I decided people wanted entertainment, so we created an absolute circus. I quit calling them games and started calling them shows."

He doubled revenue, and a new brand of baseball began.

A SHOWMAN IS BORN

In 2011, Jesse realized that he wasn't just a general manager, but a showman. He decided to embrace the role. For opening night, he got a Barnum-esque tuxedo with tails. Very classy, but it was black and drew in such an unbearable amount of heat that he "almost melted."

It was then that he ordered his first yellow tux, as an effort to keep cool. It may have looked silly, but it was also very memorable, and soon fans and others started calling him "Yellow Tux Guy." The detail stuck in the minds of the customers and connected them to the team. Since then he has built his business and brand around the simple premise of finding what makes you different. His big difference is the bold yellow that he wears (he owns seven yellow suits now, and recently his employees got a tailor to make Jesse a custom tux as a gift of appreciation), and it has certainly worked to his advantage.

While the banana-yellow tux is his brand, Cole said that "the big message is fans-first mentality. Everything we talk about is fans first. We are 100 percent committed to employees and customers." It's not just an advertising ploy; the fun yellow tuxedo makes the team's fans happy.

He went on to explain, "Love your customers more than your product and your employees more than your customers and you'll be wildly successful."

THE DIFFERENCE

To maintain the fan loyalty, Cole keeps his team relevant year-round. Their home stadium events don't end when the baseball season does.

Besides playing thirty home baseball games, the stadium hosts another thirty to fifty events: concerts, contests, races, and even beer events. In 2018, they hosted the Running of the Bananas, a 5K race to celebrate Global Running Day, where all the competitors wore banana costumes.

A particularly successful event is a morning beer festival, for which they've had 250 people line up outside at 8:30 a.m. All in a morning's work for this team. In short, they think about what is considered normal and then strive to do the exact opposite. That difference is part of what keeps them entertaining.

Their mission always comes back to the fans. What is it that the fans are there for, and how can they meet that need? For the Savannah Bananas, the answer to that is to entertain always. And it works well: the fans are passionate about the team, which serves to strengthen the resolve of the staff. They believe in their methods, which have essentially become ingrained in their DNA—a part of their inspiration.

CULTURE

As you may expect, this eccentricity creates an interesting work culture. Here is how Jesse thinks about it: "Culture is the atmosphere of your workplace. It's the culmination of your beliefs and what you stand for." The most important aspects of the Savannah Bananas culture all reflect the "Fans First Way": caring, different, enthusiastic, fun, growing, and hungry.

It is important for Cole to be aware of the culture because he knows he is responsible for it: "A leader lives and breathes the culture. They embody it with everything they do. They recognize it, encourage it, acknowledge it every day."

Though the fans may come first, it never means the employees should be neglected. The man in the yellow tux believes "a leader needs to care for others even more than you care for yourself. Be judged daily by how you care for people and make people feel."

Part of his response to this belief was to allow employees to choose how much they would make. Though this may seem like a financially dangerous move, Jesse has found that his people have not tried to take advantage of it; the average increase that his people asked for was about

22 percent, and the Savannah Bananas have been able to grant every request.

That small amount of control over their livelihoods has definitely served to increase employee loyalty. The majority of people under thirty years old leave a job every thirteen months; however, despite the fact that nearly all the staff is right out of college, in the company's first three years it had zero turnover.

MAINTAINING CULTURE: WHAT DO *YOU* TALK ABOUT EVERY DAY?

If one thing is certain, it is that this kind of successful culture only happens when it is done with intention. So how do you make it happen? Well, Savannah Bananas' leadership has several methods they use to keep their employees focused and thriving in their culture. The first is that they talk about their fans every day, keeping them first in their minds even when not interacting with them directly.

The second way has to do with recognition. Jesse feels that it is unfortunate to see how underappreciated most people are in the workplace. He opens every meeting and conversation with his president by asking, "Who are we recognizing today?" He loves to catch his people doing things right and wants everyone recognized every week or every other week.

Cole also emphasizes unity within his staff, regardless of the level. His employees have certainly witnessed his own level of commitment. Two years ago, he and his wife were suffering financially and had to sell their own house in order to invest in his dream for the team. His employees know how much he has sacrificed; they are in it together—the Savannah Bananas, regardless of whether they're selling out four thousand seats or being mocked for their fruity name.

As a company, Savannah Bananas looks for the capacity for unity and passion as early as the hiring stage. The process involves an essay on the Savannah Bananas creed, called the "Fans First Way," and a "future resume" that spells out what the applicant's dreams and goals for the future are. There is also a video cover letter and group interviews to see if the person's personality will fit with the family Savannah Bananas has become, growing from just four employees working around a picnic table to the successful organization it is now. If the staff loves the company, chances are the fans will too. The focus is always on the fans, and no one should be a bigger fan than your own employees.

Many companies expect this level of dedication from their employees, but few reciprocate. In this organization, the value placed on the staff is written into the Fans First Way: always be caring, different, enthusiastic, fun, growing, and hungry. Some of these are expected, since they improve the experience for the people who attend games and events, but traits like enthusiasm and fun are also necessary to make life tolerable and meaningful for employees. The Savannah staff works long hours, even staying until the next morning for certain events. Without passion for what they do, they would burn out quickly.

Many of these traits are difficult to train and so must be a part of the employee from the beginning, but Cole recognizes the importance of personal growth over time as well. As such, Savannah Bananas has a paid book club. That's right—the company pays the employees to read. It is yet another method that really shows how Savannah Bananas values its staff. It wants them to be ambitious—to be *hungry*—and gives them ways to satisfy the craving. Cole has even written his own book on success: *Find Your Yellow Tux: How to Be Successful by Standing Out*.[3]

PLAYERS

The players make up a side of this business that is unique. They are certainly part of the Bananas, but unlike normal employees, the rules of the NCAA state that they cannot be paid for their time. The Savannah Bananas are a summer college league, meaning that they are one of the places that amateur (college) players can still play serious baseball in a non-NCAA setting.

There are certainly some forms of compensation: the players are often hosted by fans and the like, and are provided meals as well as clothes and workout facilities. And, even better, they get to play in front of a sold-out home crowd of four thousand, a couple thousand more than a minor league team averages. However, it can also make culture a little tricky. Jesse can't "make" the college players do anything, even if he wanted to force them—he has to inspire their cooperation. Players spend their first three days learning about the Fans First system, but that doesn't mean they'll adhere to it.

When Cole brought out the choreographers in the early days, there was one player who walked off the field and refused to participate. He stayed firm on the matter until about halfway through the season, when he finally realized how much more attention the guys who were participating got from fans. Then he started to join in. The fans love the over-the-top antics, and the proof is in the pudding. Besides being the only team in the country selling out all their games, the Savannah Bananas' fans even show up just to watch *practice*.

Some players, on the other hand, fully embrace the culture from the start. One memorable example is Russell Wilson, who would go on to play quarterback for the Seattle Seahawks but first played for Cole's Gastonia Grizzlies in 2009. Instructed to give kids high-fives on the way out of the dugout, the team was about to start the game only to realize that Wilson was still running around the stands, high-fiving every kid he could reach.

EMOTION IN ACTION

The entertainment business is largely based on emotions, both for customers and staff. I asked Jesse about the emotions they are intentional about creating, both for their employees and their fans. While it is definitely important to direct the emotions of the fans to achieve the Fans First goal, Cole seems to feel that taking care of the fans creates just as strong a response in the employees, if not more so. Jesse said it best himself: "Fans First moments bring out the best emotions in our staff. After games, we talk about the amazing moments created for our fans. This often brings our staff to tears. If we can move our people to tears because of the impact we are making on others, we know we are making a difference."

Not all recognition is inspirational, but when coupled with all the other tools Savannah Bananas uses, it goes a very long way in inspiring employees. "When I asked some of our staff some of their favorite moments [being on] our team," Cole said, "I often hear that it's when we recognize them and tell them how proud we are of them. If that matters most, we as leaders look to do it as much as possible!" Which emotions do they aim for? All of those that most people would save for their families, which is what Savannah Bananas considers its employees to be.

It is not surprising then that the first emotion Jesse listed was love. He wants his people to feel loved, which then spreads naturally to the fans. Most businesses are scared of love, thinking that it may get in the way of financial gain, but not the Bananas. "I can't tell you," he said, "how many times our people have told us they love us and how many times we've told them."

Pride is another big one. Cole wants his people to feel proud of the work they are doing each day. As a group, they talk about their impact constantly so that everyone understands the difference they are making and its importance to the fans. Seeing the effects is yet another way to drive home that what they do matters and that the people in charge notice.

Cole understands the importance of gratitude and makes a point to show it. He teaches his people to write thank-you letters to fans and to always feel grateful for the opportunities they have. As previously mentioned, he shows his gratitude and appreciation for the good work done by his employees and additionally hopes that it inspires joy and happiness. He feels that if they are happier each day at work, they will feel greater purpose and make an even bigger impact. This creates fulfillment for everyone involved.

Finally, Jesse hopes that he inspires his people each day to be the best versions of themselves and push themselves to grow, develop, and never settle. Besides benefitting the company, he desires this because he values them as individuals and part of his family. As with the book club, he sees that creating an emotion and system of thinking for his employees will ultimately make them into the kind of people who will want to create these emotions for others.

WEEDING OUT THE NEGATIVE

Like weeds in a garden, negative emotions will occasionally crop up. Cole tries to protect the Bananas staff by keeping on the lookout for those emotions and finding ways to prevent them. For instance, fear and jealousy are like a worm in a piece of fruit, when what he wants is for his employees to feel safe, like a family. His people should not compare themselves and what they are doing with others; they are a team, striving for the same goals, and other teams are not doing the same things anyway.

Overall, they don't talk about negative emotions much. They focus on the positive and celebrate the good as much as possible.

INSPIRATION

Jesse Cole isn't the first leader I've encountered who uses this inspirational tool for creating success. In fact, I find it is one of the most common methods of intentional leadership: *storytelling*.

"I share stories," Jesse said. "Stories about how Fans First Entertainment was built and how we've made a huge impact on people's lives."

When you're doing things right, the experience speaks for itself: "Our culture inspires others because we truly put our employees first and our customers first. We empower our employees to have freedom with their jobs, with unlimited vacation time and the opportunity to be entrepreneurs within the business. Our group feels like they belong to something bigger than [them]selves." Telling the stories shows how they fit into the larger story.

One of the benefits of storytelling is that it either uncovers or creates the meaning and purpose people bring to their jobs, and it provides concrete examples of how they impact others. It's proof that the system is working. Cole's favorite stories show both an employee being inspired and the power of that inspiration. What follows are two of those kinds of stories, as told by Cole:

1. Keke started as a shy intern who never spoke much in the office, but we challenged her one night to sell beer at a game and be vocal. Midway through the game I saw a huge line at her beer stand and I heard her yelling, "Get tipsy with Keke!" She came out of her shell that day. I asked her what got into her and she said that she was just being herself and having fun! I told her to be like that always as that was Fans First. She then started answering the phones singing, greeting people at the door when they come into the office with a hug, and became our full-time director of first impressions. As a

twenty-three-year-old, she now oversees a staff of 150 at our games. She feels amazing purpose and is the best version of herself. She often cries when talking about her job and her impact!

2. Danny started as a sales associate, selling tickets. He began with us when no one was buying tickets and watched as we struggled to make ends meet. He persisted and was instrumental in selling out our season and raising more than $40,000 for local nonprofits. After the season, we surprised him and his dad with tickets to game one of the World Series to see their favorite team, the Cleveland Indians. He and his dad were brought to tears. Danny said he would never forget that moment and proved how "Fans First" our organization is. Danny is now vice president of our organization and leads our entire team.

Finally, Cole sees the power of inspiration in his organization when his people get emotional talking about what they do—an event that occurs regularly, to the point that many are included in the Savannah Bananas playbook.

FINAL INNING

Jesse begins his book, *Find Your Yellow Tux*, by asking what legacy the reader wants to leave. The question inspired him to write his future eulogy:

Jesse Cole was the ultimate showman who entertained millions by bringing energy, enthusiasm, and enjoyment to everything he touched. A person who inspired millions to challenge the status quo, to be different, and to live the life of their dreams. A person who truly cared for others, was always there for anyone, who would give them everything he had. And the most loving husband and father to his wife and kids. He devoted his life to them and made them happy.

That is fans and family first. That is intentional leadership.

CHAPTER 10

THE EMOTION IMPERATIVE

HOW DO PEOPLE FEEL ABOUT DOING BUSINESS WITH YOU?

"Are our blades any good? No. Our blades are f**cking great."
And so started one of the most successful marketing campaigns in recent memory. Dollar Shave Club's first YouTube commercial cost $4,500 to make and was shot in a single day. Within seventy-two hours, the ad had gone viral, ticking up millions of views and jumpstarting the start-up's rise to being an industry powerhouse.

As founder Michael Dubin, who stars in the now-famous ad, recounted:

> Our first video went live at 6:00 a.m. PT on March 6, 2012. By 7:30 a.m., the site had crashed and we couldn't get it back up for 24 hours. I was terrified that, in that moment, my biggest dreams were turning into my worst nightmares.
>
> The next day the site was back up, we had 12,000 new subscribers, and within just a few days, three million people had watched the video. Since then, we've produced another; collectively both have been viewed more than 25 million times. It was a fantastic way to come out of the gate and raise awareness of our mission. I don't think you could have accomplished that any other way.[1]

In 2016, Unilever bought Dollar Shave Club (DSC) for $1 billion.

I remember first seeing Dubin's commercial. My verdict was: *Irreverent. Edgy. And funny as hell.*

For one dollar a month, I became a subscriber—and still am. Dollar Shave Club blades are cheap, but they're not poor quality. They do what I need them to do when I shave. I also smile a little bit (at least in my mind) when I use them, remembering that first ad and the others that came after it.

The ads set a tone for the company that continues to this day, even under Unilever's umbrella. A tiny newsletter is included in each shipment, and it's always cleverly written and a joy to read. As with any good company, the newsletter pushes new product, but in a funny way—just like that original ad.

DSC was one of the first subscription companies to take advantage of the new economy. These days, you can have almost anything delivered to your door on a regular basis, but back when DSC first started doing business, it was a bit of a novelty. And it was brilliant. Convenience is key. I never have to remember to order; the box with a full month's inventory of fresh blades shows up on my doorstep.

I'm happy to be a DSC subscriber. I mean that. I smile when the box arrives; I smile when I use their product; I smile when I read the newsletter. I'm smiling right now, remembering that irreverent, hilarious first commercial the company cut seven years ago. (Seriously, if you've never seen it, stop reading right now and go check it out.)

Who'd have thought you could do all that with a razor blade? Who'd have thought that a razor-blade company could make me . . . happy?

WELCOME TO THE EMOTION ECONOMY

I've changed my mind. I used to think experience ruled, but now I believe there's a new sheriff in town.

In my book *Fred 2.0*, I explained the importance of elevating the customer experience.

I mean, what could be better than creating a great experience for your customer? Only one thing: elevating the experience so it is superior to what your competitor delivers.

I was so close . . .

But first, let's revisit the story:

I was working at an event with Jennifer Griffith, who was then the president of Commerce National Bank in Columbus, Ohio. Jennifer regaled me with a story about the time she had to placate a grumpy customer in Cincinnati, one hundred miles away. Dropping everything she was doing, Jennifer jumped into her car and started the long drive—only to have her tire blow out after twenty minutes. Then she looked at her phone—one measly bar, and she had left her charger at the office. She could call a tow truck or she could call her irate customer—she couldn't do both, and regardless, she was going to be late meeting with her customer.

She ended up calling Kevin King, the general manager of the company that had sold her, her husband, and her mother several cars. Kevin had always gone above and beyond for Jennifer, which is why his name popped into her head at that exact moment when she needed "above and beyond" to happen. Kevin rolled up with a new car, a hot cup of coffee, and a phone charger. Jennifer not only made her appointment with her customer but was also able to make calls along the way to Cincinnati.

The next day, Kevin brought Jennifer's old car directly to her office. As he was driving away, he texted her: "By the way, we washed your floor mats. They are drying in the trunk."

After recounting Jennifer's story in *Fred 2.0*, I then went on to explain the four-way test of an elevated experience:

1. the customer is surprised in a good way;
2. they are happier after the experience than before;
3. they feel they've received value; and
4. they want to tell others about their experience.

I'm not saying I was wrong. All those things remain true today, but here's the new spin, or mind shift: the elevated experience isn't the most important thing. It is a means to an end. The most important thing is how the customer *feels* about the experience.

Would Jennifer rather have not had her tire blow out, followed by her moments of panic? Absolutely. But the way Jennifer told me about Kevin, it was like she was happy to have experienced it all. She loved telling the story! It felt good to do business with someone like Kevin.

What if she had just called a tow truck? Everything might have worked out—aside from the irate customer. But we don't talk about things that meet our expectations. Your regular tow-truck company would have done what Jennifer expected it to do. I certainly never would have heard about it, because it would never have crossed Jennifer's mind to tell me.

"Oh, let me tell you about this tow-truck experience I had!"

"Was it amazing?"

"No, it was pretty average."

"Sounds riveting."

We don't recommend a movie we just like. We recommend a movie we love. Or, conversely, we talk about a movie we hated. The more positive the emotion, the more powerful the outcome.

In business we focus on outcomes, but as customers we focus on feelings. As I explained in a previous chapter, being happy after a successful business transaction is nothing new. Since the dawn of commerce, customers have wanted to feel happier after purchasing a good or service. No, the shift, caused by the new economy, is that now customers want to feel *successful* after an interaction with a company. Let's look at Jennifer. A happy experience would have been simply if Mr. Tow Truck showed up and fixed her tire (albeit making Jennifer late). That's what Jennifer expected; that's what would have happened.

But what did Kevin do? Kevin quickly brought her a loaner and got her on her way. His services allowed Jennifer to feel successful. She was able to accomplish her tasks because of what Kevin did. *That's* why she was raving about it to me. *That's* why her story made it into *Fred 2.0*.

The customer experience of success, whether it's to be happier, healthier, or more profitable or productive: *that* is what companies are now competing on—and will be in the future. And it's why I believe today we are doing business in the emotion economy: products, service, and experience are ultimately what create emotions, positive or negative. And those emotions keep us coming back and spending more or drive us into the arms of a competitor. The future of your business hinges on creating positive emotions.

I'm an economist by training, so don't think I'm advocating a weird touchy-feely concept. When a customer receives value, is pleasantly surprised by the experience, and leaves happier than when they came in, you've just scored big, because happier customers buy more, are more loyal, and—critically—tell others. I recounted my experience with Dollar Shave Club because I think it's a great story. But I also told you about it as a thoroughly satisfied customer, and I think you should give them a shot. (No, I am not being paid to write that.)

We're all too familiar with the corollary: If the customer leaves angry or upset, it is probably accompanied by a vow never to return, and they'll likely share their displeasure with your business with lots of others. Small businesses these days live or die because of online reviews: Angie's List and Yelp are just the more prominent of the review sites out there. But those same small businesses know that just meeting expectations won't result in a positive review. Only two things result in a review: an amazing experience or a terrible one.

Again, you don't recommend a movie you just liked. You recommend a movie you love—or you bash a movie you hated.

EMOTIONS EVERYWHERE

The futurist Richard Yonck was one of the first to coin the term "the emotion economy." He described it as "an ecosystem of emotionally intelligent devices and software iterations that will completely change the way we interact with machines."[2] This obviously is a bit different from what I'm referring to when I talk about the emotion economy, but both my and Yonck's definitions derive from the same shift occurring in the economy. Emotions are everywhere and they are the single biggest factor in how we make decisions.

Yonck's definition acknowledges that technology has reached a point where machines can sense human emotion. AI makes it possible to read human emotion better than most humans can. In the article "A New Kind of Currency: The Emotion Economy" by Sameet Gupte, CEO of Servion Global Solutions, Gupte said businesses increasingly use data and analysis from developing technology to read their consumers' emotions. Why? It makes sense to pay more attention to emotions because they have the potential to be very lucrative. This article reported that the market for technology that can "recognize, understand and simulate" emotions is predicted to increase to $59 billion by 2021.[3]

Facebook pioneered its platform to overtly gauge the reactions and emotions of clients (how Facebook gathered and used that data is a different topic). Another example is the MiRo robot made by Consequential Robotics. This is a companion for the elderly that is designed to gauge its users' emotions and moods so the company and, by extension, the families of the users know how the person has been feeling and can react to it.

This is just the beginning of an emphasis not on what is done or experienced but how one feels about it—that is, the emotions created. Megachurches, businesses small and large, nonprofits, and the government sector are now all creating for the same thing: share of emotion.

Regardless of whether we're talking about what machines can sense or what a customer feels, in the emotion economy, the most important question is this: How do your customers and employees feel about doing business with you?

Bain & Company has a question it uses in determining what it calls net promoter scores. It is a simple question: "On a 0–10 scale, how likely is it that you would recommend us (or this product or service) to a friend or colleague?"

That's a good question, but I think my question—if I may say so—is better:

Are you happier you did business with us than with someone else?

When someone feels really great about an experience, they tell others. When a customer feels really angry about an experience, they tell others too. When someone doesn't have strong feelings, they don't tell anyone.

Have you ever gotten a problem fixed but felt rotten about how much time it took?

Have you ever purchased a product you really liked from a person you really didn't like? You might go back to the store, but the threat of running into that pushy salesman might also keep you from doing so.

In the emotion economy, your grade isn't pass/fail. The resulting emotional state you deliver is cumulative. A negative emotional experience can be offset with a positive one.

Alan Cowen and Dacher Keltner reported that there are twenty-seven distinct categories of emotions that are interconnected with each other. These are the twenty-seven: admiration, adoration, aesthetic appreciation, amusement, anger, anxiety, awe, awkwardness, boredom, calmness, confusion, craving, disgust, empathetic pain, entrancement, excitement, fear, horror, interest, joy, nostalgia, relief, romance, sadness, satisfaction, sexual desire, and surprise.[4]

And here is where we can start to discuss intentional leadership in the emotion economy. Your customers are going to feel one of these emotions from your company. They are going to be feeling one, if not several, at many points before, during, and after their interaction with your company. The old notion that a company merely needs to provide a good or service withers away when we start to understand that it is not the product or service itself that matters—what matters is which emotion your company elicits from its customers.

Now, there's a danger of thinking way too deeply about this. Do you want your customers to be amused or entranced? Excited or satisfied? I mentioned the twenty-seven emotions only to give you a sense of the new playing field, not to break your brain in trying to decide which specific emotion is right for your customer. As you think about the emotional outcomes you create in your business, you need to be neither a linguist nor a psychologist. For purposes of intentional leadership, focus on accurate descriptions of feelings rather than trying to parse out minor differences between, say, happiness and joy.

THE EMOTIONAL LEADER

I don't want you to wear your emotions on your sleeve. Rather, I want you to understand that today's emotion economy has created an imperative for the way leaders must lead their businesses. It's likely you're already doing some of this. After all, how do you handle an angry customer? How do you capture a customer's joy? How do you ensure that your customer's expectations aren't just met but exceeded?

These are common-sense principles of business leadership. But they've also always been relegated to less-important status compared to the pillars of service and product. In the world that was, we were told to get the service and product right. That's how you competed. But in the world that is, product and service aren't enough—or, rather, our understanding of product and service has expanded, grown to include that intangible but critically important value: How do my customers feel?

Let's look back at Dollar Shave Club. Are its razors any better than Gillette's or BIC's? I have no idea. I've never done a test nor have I read a *Consumer Reports* article on which is the better blade at the better price. But I'll tell you this: I never remember smiling when I used a Gillette razor or a BIC. I never remember smiling when I purchased them. And I certainly can't tell you in any specific detail what a Gillette or BIC commercial had in it.

Dollar Shave Club was able to capture that feeling that its competitors couldn't: I felt better using its products.

The intentional leader must start to look at the totality of the customer experience, from the moment the customer first meets the company to the moment he throws the blade away—so to speak. What are your customers feeling along this continuum? What is pushing them forward? Where can you, as the leader, add to their emotional experience? Where can you induce in them a feeling of success? You don't just solve their particular problem. You make them happy that they had the problem so that you could resolve it.

That's a bit of a head-scratcher, I admit. But, again, I'm happy when I use DSC razors. Jennifer was happy that she was able to have her experience with Kevin's customer service. Gloria's parking customers are happy that they chose her lot over Bob's. You don't just want your customers to choose you; you want them to be happy that they chose you.

SIXTEEN THINGS CUSTOMERS WANT TO FEEL

As I've reviewed the literature about emotions created in service delivery, I've found that regardless of the context or research, there are primary opportunities to delight and motivate customers. Here is a list that should help you identify where, in your customer experience, you can add to their emotional experience.

1. Special: Make customers feel unique.
2. Desire: Create and fulfill their desire through showcasing.
3. Wonder: Increase their curiosity.
4. Optimistic: Help them face the future with optimism.

5. Enriched: Improve the quality of their physical or intellectual lives. Help them feel better or smarter.
6. Included: Make them feel like they're in on a secret.
7. Responsible: Encourage social responsibility for people and the planet.
8. Safe: Make them feel more secure.
9. Fulfilled: Satisfy a particular longing or desire that goes beyond basic needs.
10. Excited: Remember that you can and usually should create this emotion prior to interacting with customers.
11. Free: Make them feel like they've come to a decision on their own. No one likes a pushy salesperson.
12. Successful: Help them feel they are able to get things done, that they are more successful because they use your product, and so on.
13. Surprise: Challenge their expectations, giving them something far greater than what they imagined.
14. Passionate: Create a level of loyalty that appeals to their sense of right and wrong.
15. Loved: Make your customers feel valued and appreciated.
16. Happiness: Put your customers in a state of well-being that encompasses living a good life.

Of course, there are also emotions you want to avoid like the plague. My same research uncovered the sixteen emotions you *don't* want your customers to feel.

1. Sad: Your customer comments, "The way your manager treated the employee was disheartening."
2. Disrespected: Your customer is paying to be treated well.
3. Ignored: Your customer says, "Is anyone going to help me?"
4. Frustration: Your customer experiences call-center hell, where they can't get answers.
5. Anxiety: Your customer is left without answers and/or you are terrible at communicating.
6. Unappreciated: Your customer feels like you don't value their business.

7. Disappointed: Your customer discovers you overpromised.
8. Criticized: Your customer thinks, *Why do you have to make me feel stupid?*
9. Anger: Your customer fumes, "Your system/process/people are unhelpful and abusive."
10. Confusion: A confused customer often buys nothing or worse, the wrong thing.
11. Used: Your customer feels like doing business with you was a means to the company's end.
12. Weary: Your customer is exhausted by your company's processes and time-consuming minutiae.
13. Excluded: Your customer feels the opposite of being an insider—feeling like they don't belong.
14. Stress: Your customer feels that you are demanding and would rather leave.
15. Apathy: Your customer feels like you couldn't care less about helping them.
16. Remorse: Your customer rues the day they chose to do business with you.

HAPPY ISN'T THE ONLY EMOTION, BUT . . .

Happiness is a familiar emotion. It's the most common emotion that a customer will feel after a good experience with your company. Maybe more quickly than any other emotion, we know if we are more or less happy. In designing how you deliver emotion, consider what you can do to make customers

- happier they chose you;
- happier when they leave than when they came in; and/or
- happier overall with their lives because of you.

But happiness also results from mistakes. No company is perfect and you should be aware that how you handle a mistake also plays into a customer's happiness. Too many leaders just stop caring after their company makes a mistake. Sure, they'll do what they can to make it right, but it's almost as if they would just rather move on. Wrong. Making a mistake is an opportunity to generate a huge swell of positive emotion in your customers.

- Make 'em happy when you make a mistake . . . by solving the mistake and giving them a little extra.
- Make 'em happy when they don't buy anything . . . so that they'll come back.
- Make 'em happy when they are mad at someone else . . . by solving problems you didn't create.

Producing happiness after a mistake is an ideal way to exceed your customer's expectations. Once the mistake is made, the customer now has a negative opinion. The bar is low. Propel yourself over that bar and you just might make a loyal customer.

And sometimes the happiness or lack of happiness has nothing to do with you or your company. Nevertheless, the opportunity presents itself. A friend who works at an extraordinary restaurant related that the hostess comped a woman who was unhappy even though nothing she had experienced at the establishment warranted her attitude.

"So why did you comp her meal?" he asked.

"To help her deal with her miserable life" was the response.

While this sounds harsh, it is often the reality in dealing with the people who come into your place of work, order from you online, or call you for help. You inherit unhappy, negative customers. You didn't create the negative emotion, but it is rich with opportunity. By displacing the bad with the good that can come from doing business with you, you've created real value.

STRATEGIES FOR THE EMOTIONAL LEADER

As you start to analyze your customer service practice, keep these strategies in mind to help you prioritize. Look at each moment in the customer continuum and then

1. Decide on the emotion you want to create.
2. Defend against the emotion you want to avoid.

3. Design for emotion: structure the experience to create the desired emotion.
4. Deliver with emotion: keep the humanity in your interactions.
5. Determine experienced emotion: assess the results.

Don't forget that you can't make everyone happy all the time. Your research and analysis of your customer experience should yield results that show you who you can make happier the fastest with the least cost (and stress to you and your team).

MORE THAN CUSTOMER EXPERIENCE

If it sounds like the emotion economy is a fancy word for customer service, you're almost right. You start your journey by turning your company into one that aims to elicit specific, positive emotions from customers by first looking at your customer experience. But that's only the beginning, because a customer's emotions start well before they enter your sales funnel. They start when they see your first ad, like with Dollar Shave Club; they start when you search for a parking garage. The new economy has expanded the points at which your potential customers will first interact with your company. Across all levels of your organization, ask yourself how each impacts the customer's happiness and feelings of success. This includes marketing, product design, sales, and, yes, customer experience. It includes hiring the right people who share in your vision of adding to a customer's emotional well-being. It includes your plans for the future: How can we make customers feel even happier and more successful?

It's a never-ending journey. It starts with customer experience, but where it ends depends on your imagination.

CHAPTER 11

TEXAS ROADHOUSE

What kind of CEO displays his biggest failures on the wall of his office? Kent Taylor, founder and CEO of Texas Roadhouse, not only openly admits that three of his first five restaurants failed, but he has a memento from each mounted on the wall of his office, detailing the money lost.

"That way," he explained, "visitors can see that failure isn't a bad thing when you're trying to innovate."

THE BEGINNING

Kent Taylor lived in my home state of Colorado and worked at nightclubs and restaurants. Known as a maverick, he often "got in trouble" with chain management for his innovative ideas and promotions. He returned to Louisville, Kentucky, in 1990 with dreams of opening a Texas-themed restaurant.

His new place opened in 1993 at the Green Tree Mall in Clarksville, Indiana. Today Texas Roadhouse (TXRH) has 570 restaurants in forty-nine states and ten countries.

TXRH TODAY

Each store employs 170 to 200 team members, fondly referred to as "roadies." The 6,700- to 7,500-square-foot facilities serve steaks that are cut in-house and all made-from-scratch dishes (even the bacon bits and croutons). Their restaurants average 5,000 guests per week, and the chain serves 300,000 meals each day.

The six-ounce sirloin began as the most popular dish and remains so to this day—twenty-six years later. The steakhouse prides itself on a six-ounce cut of meat that actually does weigh six ounces, which is surprisingly rare (pun intended). Each restaurant has its own meat cutter who maintains their edge through competition. The top ten attend the company conference, and the winner is named Meat Cutter of the Year and receives a $20,000 check.

This might seem like an unnecessary expenditure to some, but an accurate cut means less wasted meat and money. The program to recognize TXRH's stars costs about $1 million, but the company estimates it saves between $10 and $20 million. It all comes back to the company's views on employees: "Embrace people and treat 'em better than they would be treated at other chains." And it certainly seems to be working.

TXRH, at the time I'm writing this, has enjoyed thirty-two consecutive quarters of positive comparable restaurant sales growth. The guest count continues to rise, 3.5 percent in the past year. The chain is about half the size of Outback Steakhouse, but is valued at more than $3 billion. Compared to that, Bloomin' Brands and its entire portfolio of restaurants—Outback, Carrabba's Italian Grill, Fleming's Prime Steakhouse & Wine Bar, and Bonefish Grill—is valued at well under $2 billion.

INTENTIONAL LEADERS ARE INVOLVED LEADERS

This kind of success doesn't happen by sitting back and letting things fall how they may.

Like so many of the leaders we interviewed for this book, Taylor is highly visible, accessible, and involved in the field.

"I was only in Louisville 102 days last year," he related. "But the best things we do at this company, I've learned from people in the field. Being involved, visiting stores, getting ideas—that is my main job. Too many times you have leaders who came out of operations as big shots and become isolated and hear what the world is through four or five people who report to them." He prefers to see things firsthand.

"I still choose all of our real estate. We've only closed three of our last five hundred Roadhouses. One reason I do the real estate is that it gives me more time in the field with people."

While he can easily be seen as a leader with a lot of great ideas, Taylor credits his team with helping him come up with and implement the best ones. "If we think about a new idea, I run it through twenty people—managing partners, market partners, kitchen managers, service managers, meat cutters. I don't create ideas in a distant office." He knows that his decisions will affect employees at all levels, so he strives to make sure those choices help rather than harm. "My job is to remove obstacles, not create them."

TXRH and its leaders have cracked the code on the emotion economy. Taylor said, "When it comes to employees, I am always asking, Are they happy? Do they enjoy their job? That's important because I believe that *happy employees create happy guests, which creates happy accountants!*" People who are happy in their work tend to spread that happiness around, which can only improve the experience for customers. Employees won't do their job as well if they are only in it for profit—it has to mean something, from dishwashing and serving to being the managing partner of the restaurant.

THEY DON'T JUST SAY "ACT LIKE AN OWNER" . . .

They make you one.

The managing partner at each Texas Roadhouse has an ownership interest in their restaurant. In exchange for 10 percent of the profits, they are required to put down a $25,000 deposit and sign a five-year employment contract. To become an area partner, or market partner, requires a $50,000 investment.

Today you also get Texas Roadhouse stock that builds in your own account, and after five years you get your investment back plus appreciated stock. It may seem like a strange setup, but Taylor sees it as a kind of test to see who has what it takes.

Why? He explained, "They have skin in the game and their name is over the front door of the restaurant. Most people don't have $25,000 sitting around, so maybe you have to borrow money from family to work for us, which separates us from our competitors, and we get people who really want to be with us." He wants potential partners to be intentional in their actions; he is not interested in those who merely join on a whim.

How you treat your work is a little like how you treat a car you own versus one you just rent. You might not think twice about driving over a pothole in a rental, but if you own the car you treat it a little differently.

TXRH CULTURE IN SIX WORDS

In a way, Taylor has a similar view of his employees. He sees people as an investment rather than a resource to be used up and disposed of. "Employees are an investment in our business, not a cost," said Taylor. Any employee who has been treated right is also a potential future guest. The same holds true for those who may not be hired, so it pays to be pleasant during interviews. After all, pleasant is part of what Texas Roadhouse looks for in an employee.

The most important phrase when it comes to this company's culture is also one that is frequently used: *Hire right, train right, treat right.*

While you can certainly teach people skills for a workplace, it is hard to train a personality. The ideal employee for TXRH is energetic and charismatic—"someone you might want to party with." Taylor feels that if you wouldn't want to spend a vacation with the applicant, why hire them? The owners select their own staff, to an extent. It comes back to the idea of having their names over the door; they are invested in each employee and even more eager for them to succeed.

That personal investment from owners actually began as a low-cost method of advertising. Before he started Texas Roadhouse, Taylor founded and co-owned Buckhead Bar & Grill, and it wasn't doing so well. He changed it around until it more closely resembled a pub, which he felt fit the clientele better. The problem was that the potential clients were not aware of the changes.

Inspiration struck when one loyal customer brought his mother in to eat one afternoon. The man had a regular radio spot, and Taylor offered him free food if he would simply talk about the restaurant while he was on the air. This seemed to go well, until the station manager paid a visit two months later. Buckhead wasn't advertising through the station, which meant they couldn't keep bringing up the restaurant. Now the manager gets free food too. Problem solved.

If Taylor could get great help by investing in time and perks for his employees, couldn't some extra consideration work to inspire loyalty in other aspects of the business? It was all a matter of maintaining a relationship where it matters, just like with owners and their hires.

TREAT THEM RIGHT

"Our managing partners who run the stores are the center of our universe," Kent said. "They don't support us; we support them, which is why our office is called the Support Center."

TXRH believes in "service with heart." That might not seem very original to the cynic, but think of all the times the service you received was vanilla and sterile. Service with heart is about injecting real emotion into what you're doing. It is about the pride of doing work for people you care about because you want to do it. It isn't obligatory, but enjoyable.

Taylor sees his restaurant as a reverse pyramid, or the Upside-Down Pyramid, as he calls it. He is the smallest section at the bottom, while the top is made up of guests, future guests, and the kitchen and service heroes who work in the business with him. While of course guests are crucial to the success of the company, this leader feels that to create the proper mind-set, you have to love your employees first and your guests second. After all, you can't really have one without the other.

GREATER PURPOSE

Another aspect of the "service with heart" culture occurs outside the restaurants. From the first store, Taylor began to ask, "What can we do to do some good in the community?" Not as a sales gimmick, but rather to instill a life lesson in his employees the way you would with your kids. He wants the Texas Roadhouse family to care about others before they care about themselves.

For instance, in 2004 a group of employees traveled to Mexico, where they rebuilt an orphanage and a community center. They had 120 restaurants at that point and made a point to arrange groups consisting of people from different states, letting them all bond as they labored together in the hot sun, proud that they were making a difference. The restaurants average four fundraisers a month for local organizations and nonprofits, resulting in over $2 million in donations.

During Hurricane Harvey, Texas Roadhouse had to temporarily close eighteen restaurants in the Houston area. But only one of those stores had sustained water damage. The others closed to the public—and left their kitchens running. The meals they made were then served out to local people in need, offered door-to-door in flooded areas, and delivered to shelters, hospitals, and first responders.

The employees who live in those areas also received financial assistance to help them meet their needs during their troubled times. The decision was made independently of area managers or corporate and cost the chain quite a bit, but they considered the efforts well worth it. Taylor sees it as yet another way that his employees are exceptional. Their generosity had an unexpected benefit as well; the loyalty showed to the customers (and noncustomers) in that area was reciprocated in a sales increase of 20 percent afterward.

CULTURE MEANS EVERYONE GETS IT

It is easy for a department or two to "get it" when it comes to culture, but often there are outliers who don't see what they do as part of the culture picture. Not so at Texas Roadhouse. At the Support Center, Puja Gatton, senior counsel of litigation and employment, explained the culture there with admirable clarity:

> Like Texas Roadhouse's signature bucket of peanuts in the front lobby, fun pictures in the hallways, in-house contests, and the thank-you notes that "roadies" send each other, the legal department's attitude is quite befitting . . . the company culture. Our company culture helps shape what we do every day and creates a more emotionally invested and more passionate workforce. It is clear that we put our money where our mouth is when it comes to treating our employees like family.

Stop reading and ask your legal counsel to explain your culture. Will their description be so flattering?

Though Texas Roadhouse pushes forward with intention, some of their starting points were happy mistakes. This is one of the aspects that particularly pleases Taylor. As someone who was often discouraged from trying out new and strange plans, he believes the freedom to make mistakes is the only way to feel safe enough to have the best ideas. If someone is punished for one less than awesome idea, why would they try to come up with a better one?

He himself has had some of his best ideas on the spur of the moment—usually in restaurants, and especially on napkins. If you ever visit the Texas Roadhouse Support Center in Louisville, Kentucky, you'll find a museum of the restaurant's history in the lobby. One of the items featured is one of the original napkins Kent Taylor used to conceptualize his business. He would have ideas while out with family or friends and needed to get them out in a concrete way before the ideas faded. Then he would pull them out the next day and tweak.

"At one point, I had a whole box of napkins," Taylor added. It just goes to show that sometimes ideas are messy—and that's the way they are supposed to be.

This probably won't be the first time you've heard this, but if you can sketch out important concepts on the back of a napkin that turn into a $3 billion company—well, that's clarity.

UNITED IN LEGENDARY

Texas Roadhouse's mission statement is "Legendary Food, Legendary Service."

Taylor came up with it in 1995, when he had five stores, three of which closed (hence the decorations in his office).

"It was a pivotal point of survival," he explained. "My original investors had given up and I needed two more investors to do store number six in Lexington, Kentucky. I had to clarify what I wanted us to look like in a simple message everyone would get. It took us ten years from the time I wrote it down until we were really nailing it on legendary food and legendary service."

Regardless of their position, Taylor hopes his employees will continually look to achieve "legendary" of their own volition. He knows that level of passion couldn't happen without proper inspiration, however. The fact that they exceed his expectations again and again shows just how proud the whole company is of their food, their community outreach, and their commitment to their Texas Roadhouse family. He knows he certainly is:

> I lead to inspire others to love their jobs and do it all with "Legendary Food, Legendary Service" as the driving force. My dream was to build a family restaurant, and not just a steak restaurant but a place where everyone could come and have a quality meal for a great value. I lead to protect what we've created over the last twenty-five years and to set us up for success long after I am gone. Success is not guaranteed—it's earned.

By instilling these values in his employees, he ensures that they can continue even when he's not around. Legendary is his legacy.

INSPIRATION

For Taylor, inspiration isn't just something you do for others, but something you do for yourself as well. He feels that "inspiration opens our eyes to possibilities and gives us a purpose to pursue our day-to-day tasks with intention and passion." Not only is it helpful, but it's essential:

> I believe inspiration fuels our motivation and gives us that "extra oomph." You can be inspired, but until you're motivated to take action, all you have are big dreams and no results. Motivation, along with a large dose of persistence, is the drive to get it done and to make it legendary because mediocrity sucks.

Taylor often talks about how important it is to be available and not to be a leader you only meet once a year at a conference. He relies on the true but often untried technique of listening way more than he talks and allowing people to not only make mistakes but celebrate them. Recognizing and celebrating employees can help inspire them to even greater accomplishments and success. Not innovation for the sake of innovation, but innovation that helps operators and improves guest experience.

As a leader, Taylor takes several steps to inspire others. He listens to feedback, making sure to keep operators at the center of the Texas Roadhouse universe. He stays "in the game," picking real estate sites, visiting stores, overseeing the menu, and generally staying involved by talking and listening to employees. As a company made up of independently owned restaurants, he promotes an entrepreneurial culture. Perhaps most importantly, he said, "I also act quickly when I see something that needs to be fixed."

WHOSE VALUES ARE CORE?

TXRH operates on four core values: partnership, passion, integrity, and fun with purpose. Surprisingly, those aren't words that Taylor chose.

"I didn't come up with those words," Taylor said. But before we explain how TXRH arrived at these values, you need to know about the fall listening tour:

> We do a fall listening tour to twenty-some cities to interact with managing partners, market partners, kitchen managers, service managers, the team. We'll meet with folks and take notes based on this question: How can I make life better for you in your store? The listening tour allows the men and women running the restaurants to have a voice and signifies a true partnership. We also believe that empowered people have more passion for the business.

So back to those four values. During one fall listening tour they asked managing partners and others to suggest what they believed were the core values of TXRH.

"When we got back to the Support Center," Taylor explained, "we put about one hundred of those values on the board and gave people a chance to add their own. We then voted and ranked them to see what the most important values were."

Last year on the fall tour, Kent and Scott were meeting with Bubba's 33 (their newest concept). The managing partners raised some concerns that were then discussed in the meeting. However, Taylor didn't think that was good enough, so in the following two weeks, he called every attendee personally to discuss the issue. Impressive, but here's the bigger point: he acted on what he learned.

"If you listen and don't take action," he said, "you're full of shit."

THE CODE FOR ROADHOUSE CULTURE

Not only does culture shape behavior and results, Taylor believes, but "culture binds us all together. It's how we treat others, how we put our core values into action, and it's the vision that unites us. We say our culture is by design, not default."

Intentional leaders are clear on the primary drivers of their culture, and Taylor is no exception. He said the TXRH levers are:

1. vision based on core values;
2. people who embody that culture;
3. opportunity for growth, both financially and emotionally;
4. outreach through service, relationships with the guests and their communities, rather than advertising; and
5. staying true to their roots.

Even more significant, each of these values is evident in the decisions that have shaped the company through the years.

INSPIRATION MEANS CELEBRATING WHAT HASN'T CHANGED

Kent Taylor believes you inspire not just with the new and exciting but by continually acknowledging and celebrating what hasn't changed. At TXRH this includes:

- Compensation. The practice of paying in $25,000 and receiving 10 percent of profits has never changed. Other chains began with a similar model and infamously cut it back when managers started making too much money—in their opinion.

- Managers control hiring. Let managers bring in their own people to clear up the issue of accountability. They are responsible for any good or bad hires and are left to decide if these people are "eagles" or "ducks." (Eagles soar to great heights, while ducks flock together and poop all over the place.) From that point, the next step is clear: "We shoot ducks and hire eagles, or they will mess with the culture."
- Make mistakes. Give leaders the freedom to spread their wings and try new things.

Many organizations I've worked with have struggled to balance "staying true to their roots" and innovating. I asked Taylor how that affected progress. He responded that innovation is one of their roots:

> I've consistently told the same message for twenty-five years, but always been open to good ideas coming from our restaurants. Years ago, in Ashland, Kentucky, managing partner Neal Niklaus decided he was going to try line dancing in the store. I heard about it, went to see it, thought it was really cool. Since I was receptive, Neil—who is now a regional market partner—would tell me any time he had a good idea. I would tell him to give it a try.

Line dancing has since become a trademark in most of the TXRH restaurants.

The innovations go on and on, from stores all over the country. One location initiated Alley Rally, which is a preshift meeting or a sort of mini pep assembly, where an employee can create their own chant, winning the opportunity to "cash and dash."

One restaurant set out to host a coloring contest for children, only to create a new mascot for the chain. Reluctant to have the children associate the longhorn with their dinner, an employee decided to use a more unique animal, and so Andy the Armadillo was born. There's even an armadillo costume, which Kent himself wore to the state fair.

Another started using a "manager in the window" rather than an employee to inspect all food before it headed out, and the food began outperforming other locations.

Damn, that's a good idea! Taylor thought, and took it another step, hiring product and service coaches for locations. He doesn't like to take credit, though. Even when he comes up with the idea, he finds a store to try it out, and if it works well, then it "started in that store."

He loves when roadies and future employees are innovative. When Steve Miller—now a market partner—came to interview, he came with a trophy, which read:

Resume of Steve Miller

To Kent Taylor:
Don't put me on the shelf,
Choose me as the leader
Of your second concept

Kent didn't even have the second concept at the time, but he still has the trophy. He embraces creative people like Steve, who has a high-energy personality and loves others. They are the people who will spread the values of Texas Roadhouse.

"We want to make every decision, both big and small," he said, "with our food, service, and people in mind."

This ties into the "shared-ownership mentality" that employees must have to keep the culture thriving. This doesn't just apply to actual owners; the vision is to empower employees in knowing they are the keepers of the company's culture. Their actions and values determine the future of the company.

HOW DO YOU CREATE LEGENDARY CONNECTIONS AND POSITIVE EMOTIONS?

It begins with employees: Taylor wants you to be inspired before he even hires you.

"In the interview," he said, "we ask: What are you passionate about? We want to hear good answers and hear excitement." If you don't have passion in your own personal life, how can you muster any for your work?

"I remind people," Taylor continued, "to look in the mirror every morning and to monitor how you are going to look when you walk into work. You may think you are happy, but you might need to notify your face." Emotions pass from employees to customers; how will you influence the people you are helping?

The relationship between the employees and the guests has always been essential to the emotions created during the interaction. A positive vibe, great food and service, and emotional contact all contribute to that relationship; if one is off, the whole experience could be ruined for that guest.

To improve the chance of a great visit, Texas Roadhouse has decreased the number of tables each employee takes care of to three, even as competitors have increased that number to as high as six. This means TXRH servers will never have to focus on more than fifteen people at a time.

Taking care of fewer guests means consistently better service. The servers introduce themselves by name, learn the customers' names (written on the ticket if necessary), compliment their kids or spouse, and generally create a more positive vibe. Besides improving the service itself, Texas Roadhouse has found a way to establish a relationship. Now their guests come in for their fix of atmosphere and fun.

In the past, investors have encouraged the company to expand into lunch, but Taylor has refused. Much of the appeal lies in the energy provided by the staff. Being able to run one shift a day means the food is fresher and employees can run one great shift rather than a full day. For many of these people, this will only ever be a part-time job, but that doesn't mean their experience is any less important. Twenty-six years in, they find that many of the people who worked with them for three years have become lifetime guests.

TXRH MONITORS EMOTION

Every interaction with a guest is an opportunity to create an emotion, either good or bad. Intentional leaders take active steps to make good ones and to circumvent the bad ones.

"Walk into one of our stores," Taylor encouraged. "Were you greeted with a smile? Do our employees seem to be having fun? How's the energy level? Table visits are an operational goal at Texas Roadhouse; our managers check in to make sure our guests are enjoying legendary food and legendary service." Keeping track of the current emotions allows you to predict future emotions and influence them through your actions.

The same holds true for keeping employees in an infectiously good mood. Texas Roadhouse receives feedback on every level: one-on-one to 360 degrees to their annual fall listening tour—just a few ways the company keeps its finger on the pulse of how employees are feeling at any given time.

In addition, the company is always listening to reviews from customers through guest relations and social media. They work to correct any circumstance of negative emotions for guests and celebrate positive guest feedback through company-wide communications and in Alley Rallies. Texas Roadhouse knows that those connections are imperative:

> As a family restaurant, we want our guests to enjoy an authentic experience with their families and friends through their interactions with our employees. Part of that authentic experience includes giving our employees the training and support they need to be proud of their job.
>
> We want to avoid feelings of insignificance and feeling powerless. Every interaction we have, whether it be with a guest or with a fellow roadie, we want our interactions to be authentic and genuine. As part of our local approach and people-first culture, our operators, store employees, and Support Center employees all have the opportunity to take ownership over their jobs to make a difference in their own way.
>
> Once again, *happy employees create happy guests, which creates happy accountants*!

Good emotions are self-perpetuating.

THROW A PARTY

For those hoping to follow him in the ways of an intentional leader, Kent Taylor offered this advice:

Here's what I say whenever I speak and to any business I speak to: hire friendly, outgoing, and passionate. Every day we're throwing a party in our restaurants. If you're going to throw a great party, you make sure the lighting is right, the air-conditioning is adjusted, the music is great, the food you serve your guests is great, and make sure you have enough cold beer. You can relate any business to this.

You have to love where you are at, know you are doing good things for people, that the training you've gotten helps you show you care. You care about your people, and you care about your mission, your people, and your customers. Everyone wants to feel loved and part of a group. And everybody loves a great party.

Taylor's vision for the future is that the party will go on with or without him—and that it will continue to be legendary.

CHAPTER 12

ENVISIONING GREEN

When Steven Johns started mowing lawns at the age of twelve, he never imagined the summer job would grow into an entire lawn care company. Four years later, he hired another person part-time. By his senior year of high school, Steven had taken enough classes that he could leave by 1:00 p.m. every afternoon to work.

Back then, Steven mowed up and down his street, enjoying the freedom that earning money afforded him. His wife, Erika, joined the team in 2013, and today Envisioning Green is a husband-and-wife-owned, boutique-style landscape construction and maintenance company being featured in a business book.

I first met the couple while speaking at an event. I instantly connected with their gregariousness, love of life, and desire to learn and grow their business, but it wasn't until some years later that I visited their operation and my suspicions were confirmed.

KEEPING CLARITY

You can often judge the success of a company by the style and substance of its leaders, and it was easy to see that Envisioning Green is a standout company in what is often a tired and uninspired green business. The difference? Both Erika and Steven understand the power of clarity in their company: "Clarity to us is like success," they agreed. They know that you don't really get one without the other.

However, the couple also knows that it is not something you ever really achieve. Clarity is an ongoing process: "Just because you've achieved it today doesn't mean that it's going to be as clear tomorrow. You must always be striving for clarity in what you do and how you speak to your team." This doesn't make the effort futile by any means; it just makes your efforts all the more important. Even if perfect clarity may never really be achieved, the owners of Envisioning Green still believe that a certain level of it can be maintained.

"You know you've achieved clarity when the systems you've put in place work without needing [your] direct assistance. And when the decisions that [our] team makes are filtered through the same filters and four values we built our business on, we know we've been successful." This can require a certain amount of creativity because the Johnses recognize that clarity for one person may not be the same for another. It is obvious that they value their employees as individuals, rather than simply a means to an end.

THE BEST PART OF YOUR DAY

They place the same value on everyone they encounter: "One thing we always say is 'Be the best part of everyone's day,' and it's awesome when someone takes that to heart." This principle is also evident in the other key elements of their founding beliefs.

While most companies adhere to the 80/20 rule, Envisioning Green tries to include the whole team in the training process, rather than most of the training being done by a small portion of the staff. *All* the staff should have the same enthusiasm as a recruiter so that the core values are instilled in new employees early. Steven and Erika hire for attitude and train for skill. If someone is really qualified but is terrible to be around, they won't be a good fit.

WHAT'S IN A RELATIONSHIP?

The care that is put into training employees inspires their loyalty, an aspect important to the business's survival, but no less impressive for that.

The green business is generally considered a seasonal role, which means that employees are often left with little or no work during the off season. This can endanger the stability of their home lives, and many will find other work to keep themselves afloat. While necessary, it means that the business loses many employees from year to year.

Envisioning Green responded by finding methods to keep these employees working through the off season as well. They built a second warehouse to fabricate materials for orders or high-use items (kitchens, fireplaces, firepits) for future jobs. This creates productive work through February, preparing for their home show in March. Though keeping their employees busy year-round has occasionally put them in tough straits financially, they feel that having high-quality help during their busy seasons is worth it, especially since they rely on experienced workers to help push their product.

Much of their business relies on what they call "relationship marketing." In short, charisma and quality work make them pleasant to work with, and when combined with the fantastic results, customers are generally eager to tell others. For example, a job Envisioning Green completed three years ago led to six new customers. One of these was the president of a different business who was visiting the original customer and who was so impressed with what he saw that he asked them to come work on his building too—several states away.

PLANTING THE SEEDS OF INSPIRATION

Just as often, however, that trust will be created through an interaction with a passionate employee. One in particular came to mind for Steven and Erika: "Planter Pete," as he is affectionately known, frequently impresses potential clients with his unwavering enthusiasm for his work. A perfect example of the "hire for attitude, train for skill" concept, Peter is inspired to make people feel good, and the people he interacts with sense it and respond in kind. On one occasion, a couple made a $106,000 proposal after a single conversation with Peter at the home show. He is frequently requested by name, and Erika and Steven recognize that this is a direct result of his inspiration showing through. Here is an example of the kind of feedback Envisioning Green gets about Peter:

To: Steven Johns
From: Michael Lawrence

Envy is not something most wear well but, when around Peter, all have to wear it at some point. C'mon, the guy is simply blessed in too many ways. He's one of the truly fortunate few who works in a field he loves, works at a company he loves, and works with people he loves. How many of us in all the world get to enjoy that on a daily basis?

And while many who are in a position where required to meet and cater to a multitude of customers might tend to become a bit jaded over time, Peter is totally the opposite. He thoroughly embraces and promotes Envisioning Green's policy of total customer satisfaction. It all sounds a bit over the top, but it's true.

Peter is creative, talented, and completely sincere; even repeatedly thanks his customers for their giving him the opportunity to create something special for them regardless of whether they have just perhaps hit him with the 32nd change in what they want done. He actually seems to thrive on the challenges when the rest of us would be pulling our hair out or silently screaming.

While Peter's business title simply reads Horticulturalist, he's also a landscape designer and, when necessary, serves to fill a multitude of other positions; does everything from taking a position on a snow-shoveling crew in winter to acting as the official fire twirler at company customer-appreciation events held several times throughout the year.

Understand that Peter is just one of the many team members, or "family," at Envisioning Green. Each has their own unique set of skills and experience, but all, like Peter, seem to take exceptional pride in what they do and display a degree of excellence in workmanship that I have, too often, thought long since lost in this age of "good enough."

Steven Johns, the ever-hands-on owner of EG, also deserves a side note of praise in that he has brought together such people who so easily share a strong work ethic and appreciation for one another. It's not always easy, as a boss or supervisor, to correctly identify each employee's strengths and weaknesses, and know how to place them together to form a truly viable, reliable workforce; no small feat that he's done it. I would hope he is proud of both himself and all those he's chosen as "family."

Now about my project's 33rd change . . .

To inspire others, you need to be inspired. Steven's inspiration lies in legacy; he hopes that he will be remembered as a leader with a positive impact—a builder of people who makes a difference in others' lives. Erika also wants to be a positive influence. She loves people and believes in them, but just as importantly, she wants them to live with a purpose, secure in the knowledge that someone believes in them. Thus inspired, the couple tries to make sure that their employees are similarly impassioned.

"We make sure that our people know that we're grateful for them," they explained. This is done through handwritten thank-you notes, constant expressions of gratitude and pats on the back, and by praising them openly. They encourage and reward creative thinking both with customer experience and on jobsites. The track for success is clearly outlined for ambitious employees to see where to focus their efforts in order to progress; the Johnses even provide training events and both professional and personal speakers. However, Envisioning Green knows that a healthy business needs more than just financial drive—it needs human connection.

MAINTAINING CULTURE

"Our culture is fun and positive," Erika said. "We aren't afraid to laugh and joke around but we know how to work hard. You spend more time with your coworkers than your family a lot of the time, so it's important to have some fun at work." The couple aspires to a culture of joy, hard work, and contagious positivity, and designed theirs with that in mind. The culture of their intention is one in which each person feels confident in their identity as part of the company and knows how to act—not because it's the "rule," but because they genuinely believe it's the right thing to do.

Trainees who come in with the right attitude have these values instilled in them by similarly inspired seasoned employees who go above and beyond because they want to, not because they are told.

The goal is for a kind of family setting with fun as a key point. Their business is hard and intensive work, so it helps to keep the attitude light and airy. As such, they hold several events throughout the year and invite their employees to bring their own families in and enjoy themselves. The holiday party is always fun—arcade games and laser tag have been main activities in the past—and it helps the employees see the people they work with as real people, not just employers and coworkers.

It's important for the families to be involved because they affect the overall contentedness of the employee; if their family isn't happy, then they aren't happy. The employee knows that with Envisioning Green, their family comes first. If something comes up at home, their company will help them sort it out.

Steven and Erika also hold monthly breakfast meetings, which they have catered. They do follow an agenda to keep everyone up to date on what is going well and what is not, adding in positive testimonies and examples, but they also try to keep it fun with a game called Bean Boozle. Everyone receives tickets, which are then put into a drawing. The person who is picked must answer a question about the company or give an example of someone who demonstrated a core value. If they get the answer wrong, they have to eat a jelly bean, which are of a variety that could be anything from fruit to dog food. If they get the answer correct, however, they get to pick another person to go.

It's a great method to equalize individuals. No one is off limits to choose, and Steven in particular is chosen a lot. He's there to play the game too, after all. Everyone sits mixed in together at level tables to rehearse the core values. The meeting then helps everyone feel comfortable at work. They know they can talk to Steven or Erika if they have a problem, and the couple will be considerate of their emotions.

CULTIVATING EMOTION

After all, Envisioning Green's system is designed to deliver positive emotions. Most leaders have never asked themselves which emotions they are trying to create and which they are trying to avoid. Steven and Erika, on the other hand, are quite clear on which emotions they hope to create in both employees and clients.

Employees		Clients	
Positive to create	*Negative to avoid*	*Positive to create*	*Negative to avoid*
Fulfillment	Frustration	Appreciation	Frustration
Appreciation	Disappointment	Peace of mind	Anxiety
Love	Indifference	Trust	Disappointment
Joy	Delusion	Joy	Delusion
Importance		Excitement	

Interestingly enough, the lists for both employees and clients are fairly similar. The emotions fit well with the idea of being the best part of everyone's day, joy and appreciation especially. Envisioning Green has its own way of doing this with customers. A significant aspect of creating positive emotions with clients is maintaining professionalism, a problem that many other companies in the green business struggle with (e.g., not answering the phone, not returning calls, a general lack of communication, and more).

Envisioning Green aims to provide a professional customer experience from beginning to end. Rather than other landscapers, they consider their competition to be high-end businesses such as Mercedes or Fleming's. Creating positive customer emotions is therefore imperative. This is not necessarily an easy concept to put into action, however, especially if the client is predisposed differently.

Steven recalled an instance of a client who was particularly tough—not very open to being friendly with the people working on his yard and just generally cranky. He may have had other factors contributing to this attitude that the employees from Envisioning Green did not know about, perhaps the loss of a loved one or a difficult situation at his own job, but all the employees could do was go about being their normal friendly and helpful selves and hope that the client would loosen up with repeated doses of kindness.

After a month of terrible behavior, the client came out as someone was loading incorrect materials, and he began yelling. Not a great situation. However, once he found out that the error had occurred at the business who had sent the material, rather than with the order put in by Envisioning Green, his entire demeanor changed. He was suddenly much nicer; he started chatting with the workers and asking about their weekends. Sometimes it may feel like talking to a wall with some clients, but people are listening, and they do appreciate a task well done, even if you don't find out about it until later.

WE CAN TOO

You hear the refrain frequently and maybe you've used it yourself: *Sure, that works for them, but not for us.* I included this example of a small business as proof that intentional leadership isn't just for the large or the corporate but for any business that aspires to thrive and grow. Try taking the sentiment and turning it around: *If they can do it, then maybe we can too.*

DON'T FALL
DOWN THE STAIRS

I've had two clients who, to my way of thinking, were a bit obsessive about using handrails.

I was speaking to the leaders of Union Pacific in Omaha and went onstage to do a sound check. The riser was twenty-four inches high, and when I finished I jumped down from the stage.

An executive in the front row motioned me over with a solemn expression. After introducing himself as the head of safety, he politely but firmly asked me to use the handrail going on and offstage.

"Our people are required to do the same, and we don't want you to set a bad example." I didn't outwardly roll my eyes, but I thought it was a bit much. I did, of course, respect his wishes.

When speaking for Noble Oil on a different occasion, the same request was made. Not without a small chuckle, I once again honored the request. I couldn't help but feel these people were creating an issue out of nothing.

Then, several months later, I descended the stairs in my home one morning with my five-pound dog in one arm and my laptop in the other. Without the rail to support me, I slipped on the last step and—in an effort to save the dog and computer—went down hard on my right hip and arm. Nothing was broken, but it was several days before the pain eased up and several weeks before the bruising disappeared.

Now I see the logic for using the railing.

Regrettably, I didn't learn from my clients who understood basic safety far better than I did. I had to tumble down the stairs myself before I became a believer.

As an author, I know you can read a book and roll your eyes at some suggestions. And sometimes for good reason. But when it comes to intentional leadership and the simple yet powerful concepts it is built on, I hope you don't have to take that fall before you practice them.

Not learning from those who have good ideas and seasoned experience is to invite a fall down the stairs of business. You know what needs to be done, but you don't do it—until the ground starts to slip out from under you. You might not even realize it's happening; a fall can come in many forms.

Maybe last month's priorities suddenly got derailed by a new priority, and past commitments to direction are out the door.

Maybe you are struggling to figure out how to manage a new generation in the workforce when carrot-and-stick motivation doesn't work.

Customer service that used to be considered exceptional is suddenly ordinary and you're noncompetitive. Perhaps you're missing out on the emotion economy.

Culture might still seem like something you know is important, but you missed the step when it comes to designing and creating it.

A few stumbles may happen, but you need to learn to readjust; the world that is can change quickly. From clarity to culture to emotion, there are new challenges. Some businesses are adapting rapidly but most are being left behind.

The elements of intentional leadership that I've outlined in this book are—I firmly believe—necessary not just to survive but to thrive and prosper in the world as it is.

IMPERATIVES ARE ALWAYS AN IMPROVEMENT

Let's say you quibble with what I'm calling imperative. You have your own argument for how companies that aren't effectively using inspiration, culture, and/or emotion are getting by—and in some rare instances, actually thriving.

Even if you believe that—and obviously I am convinced differently—you'd have a difficult time disputing that a healthy, well-designed culture isn't a big improvement over an average, by-default culture.

You'd be hard pressed to prove that inspired work isn't an improvement over the get-it-done work often produced by a bare-minimum kind of culture, or that employees inspired by a higher purpose aren't an improvement over those motivated only by a paycheck.

Likewise, positive emotions—feeling good about doing business with a company and the loyalty it brings—are a vast improvement over "I'll do business there until a better opportunity comes along."

You see my point. What I call imperative is decidedly an upgrade over the usual way of doing business. Maybe you can get by without treating them as imperatives, but why wouldn't you at least aspire to the advancements they bring?

REALITY BLUEPRINTS

Envisioning Green is a well-loved mom-and-pop landscaping company that started with a twelve-year-old's aspiration in his backyard. Acuity Insurance is a large company in a business generally considered stodgy but that exemplifies loyalty and has fun doing it. The Savannah Bananas are a small team in a small league with a franchise-size following. High Point University represents a typical American success story—from small and struggling to popular and thriving. Texas Roadhouse is a huge restaurant chain that began as the brainchild of a man who was bounced around from places like KFC and Bennigan's. Success can come in all shapes and sizes and—even more importantly—great leadership can make it happen.

WHAT CONCLUSIONS CAN YOU DRAW FROM THESE CASE STUDIES?

Most of these businesses have built their cultures from scratch, either because it was a new business (TXRH and Envisioning Green) and/ or because the leader knew the current model was not working (HPU,

Acuity, and Savannah Bananas). Culture-building and maintenance is job number one for the intentional leader.

These leaders, whether founders or successors, carefully defined their brand promise, their first principles, their organization's raison d'être. While there were changes that came from learning and growth, they never wavered from their clarity of what the organization was about and sought to represent the changes they wanted to see.

The leaders' accessibility, visibility, and connection with employees are primary drivers of both motivation and the work being done. Nobody in these organizations studies or works harder than the leader, and it inspires team members to turn in their best performances as well.

These leaders know that the happiness of the employees affects the happiness of customers. They realize that employees are also customers and that there are no better advocates or advertising than inspired, happy employees. Many businesses emphasize the importance of placing customers before yourself, but the ones led by intentional leaders see the additional layer: employees > customers > you.

Each of these leaders truly values and invests in their employees. They hired for culture and fit, knowing that skills can be taught later.

All know that how people feel—about their education, their workday, their experience—trumps all. Creating a positive experience isn't left to chance. These organizations design and deliver for positive emotions and make a great effort to avoid the negative ones.

They don't settle for the simple motivational shtick of yesteryear, and you shouldn't either. Inspiration has a necessary place in the business world that is.

Thirty Things They Do That You Can Do Too

1. Crystallize your primary reason for being.
2. Make sure all your messaging, meetings, processes, and policies support your primary objectives.
3. Talk about what's important incessantly.
4. Prioritize what is important to you, your employees, and your customers.

5. Own what is good and what needs improvement; delusions will get you nowhere.

6. Use newsletters, emails, or any effective form of communication to keep employees informed and inspired.

7. Know that good businesses *adapt* to new improvements and information; tradition should not keep you stagnant. Tradition and innovation can and must exist together.

8. Listen to your employees as much as to your customers; allow suggestions to come from any department for any other department. There should be no criticism for keeping others on task.

9. Be available and approachable. Encourage questions from everyone.

10. Educate employees right from the start about what matters at your company.

11. Provide the skills-training employees need to succeed in their roles.

12. Model expected behavior.

13. Recognize your employees with both words and gifts for the good they do.

14. Value employees and treat them well, and they will do the same for customers.

15. Foster positive interactions with potential employees or customers (no matter how young).

16. Continually emphasize purpose and why it is important.

17. Support the causes you and your employees believe in.

18. Design compensation so employees have skin in the game.

19. Define your culture. Start from scratch if necessary but don't accept culture by default.

20. Hire for culture, train for skills.

21. Train culture through formal education, frequent meetings, and activities.

22. Plan for fun, budget for fun, and *have* fun.

23. Celebrate staff and their ideas continually.

24. Tell stories about the mission lived as a business and as individuals.

25. Value and love your employees like family.

26. Remember that your legacy will last only as long as the passion of the people under you.
27. Monitor how employees feel about working with you.
28. Don't just aim for familiarity. Make connections.
29. When employees get a say in things, they care more about them.
30. Design for and deliver position emotions.

The Six Big Questions of Intentional Leadership

Question 1: *Are you doing business in the world that is?*

What are you doing now that isn't working as well as it once did? Do you constantly monitor the routines of your work to make sure they don't turn into ruts?

Are key leaders coasting toward retirement, convinced they have no reason to change or update since they are short-timers?

Question 2: *Are you absolutely clear about your top priorities and reason for being?*

Does everyone understand job number one in your company? Or do you waffle from day to day or month to month about your primary objectives?

Remember: *You can only hit a target you can't see by accident*—and rarely at that.

Question 3: *Are you and your team taking appropriate action every day to achieve those top priorities and fulfill your mission's mandate?*

Have you assessed behaviors of every employee in every department to make sure that they are moving everyone toward the desired objectives? Or do you have organizational drag caused by people spending too much time doing low-priority (or wasted) work?

Question 4: *Have you designed and maintained the right kind of culture?*

Culture is critical. If inspiration is the fuel, culture is the engine that drives results. Intentional leaders choose and create the right culture.

Question 5: *Are you effectively inspiring your team?*

Motivation is good, but it isn't enough. Employees today want purpose infused into their work.

Question 6: *Are you designing and delivering what customers want in the emotion economy?*

The emotion economy puts a premium on how customers feel about doing business with you. Experience is wasted unless it creates the right kind of positive emotions and avoids the wrong ones.

If you can answer those questions affirmatively, that's great. But can those you lead do the same?

The Intentional Team Test

Ask your employees these six questions:

1. What is the top priority we are trying to achieve?
2. Why?
3. What actions do you take every day to achieve it?
4. Describe our culture.
5. Are you engaged, motivated, or inspired in your work?
6. What emotion best describes how you feel at the end of each day?

INTENTIONAL LEADERSHIP REVISITED

So what will you do now?

Maybe you need to rewind your leadership, to revisit what you're trying to do or even why you are trying to do it. Here are some thoughts to keep in mind:

- Be brutally honest about whether you're doing business in the world that was or the world that is.

- Apply yourself stringently to doing those things that move you toward your goals.
- Consider your purpose and the purpose you can offer those on your team.
- Don't tolerate those who go against culture, but revere those who support and contribute to it.

All the information in the world won't help if you do not act on it. Knowing is only half the battle; prepare for the next step to better business.

LEAD INTENTIONALLY

Consider the best leaders you have worked with and for. What did each of them have in common? They produced desired results, certainly. But what made those results—and the means used to achieve them—matter? They mattered because they made your life better. You weren't just a better employee or an improved means to an end. You were a valued contributor who felt like going to work every day was more than just obligatory. It was the chance to present your best self to the world, to do good work, and make a difference in a way that positively affected others.

When you think about it, leaders create a virtuous cycle; they make your life better and you make the lives of your colleagues and customers better.

Whether you are cutting meat, mowing lawns, managing a claim, teaching a college student, or putting on a show disguised as a baseball game, you make life better for others.

And a better life—isn't that what anyone, anywhere, wants and needs?

Intentional leadership is a means to that end. Using the imperatives of culture, inspiration, and emotion, you have the tools you need to make that happen.

So get clear on that and get started.

Lead intentionally.

ACKNOWLEDGMENTS

Thanks to:

Blake Dvorak, a great resource and writing collaborator.

Anna Bouwkamp for her research assistance.

My literary agent and valued friend Matt Yates.

The team at HarperCollins Leadership, who are a pleasure to work with.

My friend and business partner Peter Lynch for his feedback.

Darla, my wife, for more than I can list.

The leaders at Acuity, Envisioning Green, High Point University, the Savanah Bananas, and Texas Roadhouse, who freely shared their experiences and wisdom.

NOTES

Chapter 1: A Question I Couldn't Answer
1. Emphasis added.
2. https://addicted2success.com/quotes/36-intriguing-quotes-by-ingvar-kamprad/.
3. Quoted in Terence Irwin, *Aristotle's First Principles* (New York: Oxford University Press, 1988), chap. 1.

Chapter 2: Intentional Leadership, Defined
1. James F. Peltz, "Domino's Pizza Stock Is Up 5,000% since 2008. Here's Why," *Los Angeles Times*, May 15, 2017, https://www.latimes.com/business/la-fi-agenda -dominos-20170515-story.html.
2. Kyle Wong, "How Domino's Transformed into an E-commerce Powerhouse Whose Product Is Pizza," *Forbes*, January 26, 2018, https://www.forbes.com/sites /kylewong/2018/01/26/how-dominos-transformed-into-an-ecommerce-power house-whose-product-is-pizza/#c919de47f761.
3. Wong, "How Domino's Transformed into an E-commerce Powerhouse."
4. Chase Purdy, "Domino's Stock Has Outperformed Google, Facebook, Apple, and Amazon This Decade," Quartz, March 22, 2017, https://qz.com/938620/dominos -dpz-stock-has-outperformed-google-goog-facebook-fb-apple-aapl-and-amazon -amzn-this-decade/.

Chapter 4: The World as It Is
1. Debbie Haski-Leventhal and Mehrdokht Pournader, "Business Students Willing to Sacrifice Future Salary for Good Corporate Social Responsibility: Study," SmartCompany, February 23, 2017, https://www.smartcompany.com.au/people -human-resources/business-students-willing-sacrifice-future-salary-good-corporate -social-responsibility-study/.

Chapter 5: High Point University
1. "Press Kit," High Point University, accessed March 12, 2019, http://www.highpoint .edu/presskit/.
2. "Press Kit," High Point University.
3. "Data Shows 97 Percent of HPU Graduates Are Employed or Furthering Their Education Within 6 Months," High Point University, February 6, 2019,

http://www.highpoint.edu/blog/2019/02/data-shows-97-percent-of-hpu
-graduates-are-employed-or-furthering-their-education-within-6-months/.

4. Tom Peters and Robert H. Waterman, *In Search of Excellence: Lessons from America's Best-Run Companies* (New York: Harper and Row, 1982).

5. Annika Hom, "Employers Seek More Emotionally Intelligent Hires," *Boston Globe*, February 7, 2019, https://www.bostonglobe.com/metro/2019/02/06/employers-seek -more-emotionally-intelligent-hires/PuXiZXaHybshlODWMkc38I/story.html.

6. "High Point University Ranking Indicators," *U.S. News & World Report*, accessed March 5, 2019, https://www.usnews.com/best-colleges/high-point-university-2933 /rankings.

7. "Press Kit," High Point University.

Chapter 6: The Culture Imperative

1. "2014 Word of the Year: Culture," *Merriam-Webster*, accessed March 5, 2019, https://www.merriam-webster.com/words-at-play/2014-word-of-the-year.

2. Lara Callender Hogan, *Designing for Performance: Weighing Aesthetics and Speed* (Sebastopol, CA: O'Reilly Media, 2015), 135.

3. Mirja Telzerow and Ira Gaberman, "Cracking the Culture Code: How Organizations Get Where They Want to Go," A.T. Kearney, 2015, https://www .atkearney.com/leadership-change-organization/article?/a/cracking-the-culture -code-how-organizations-get-where-they-want-to-go.

4. Wikipedia, s.v. "immune system," accessed March 5, 2019, https://en.wikipedia .org/wiki/Immune_system.

5. "FedEx Attributes Success to People-First Philosophy," FedEx, accessed March 5, 2019, http://www.fedex.com/ma/about/overview/philosophy.html.

6. Liz Pellet, "Importance of Culture" (infographic) in Josh Bersin, "Culture: Why It's the Hottest Topic in Business Today," *Forbes*, March 13, 2015, https://www .forbes.com/sites/joshbersin/2015/03/13/culture-why-its-the-hottest-topic-in -business-today/#2982bc0f627f.

7. Gallup, "Do Employees Want What Your Workplace Is Selling?" in "State of the American Workplace," 2017, https://www.gallup.com/workplace/238085/state -american-workplace-report-2017.aspx.

Chapter 7: Acuity Insurance

1. "100 Best Companies to Work For: 2017," *Fortune*, http://fortune.com/best -companies/2017.

2. Based upon Acuity's 2018 survey of its insured claimants.

3. "Acuity Zombie Apocalypse," video, 4:00, YouTube, April 17, 2015, https://www .youtube.com/watch?v=GWNXx0rByHk.

Chapter 8: The Inspiration Imperative

1. https://nhimapparel.com/.

2. Jack Zenger and Joseph Folkman, "What Inspiring Leaders Do," *Harvard Business Review*, June 20, 2013, https://hbr.org/2013/06/what-inspiring-leaders-do.

3. Findings from the Quality of Life @ Work study, conducted from November 2013 to June 2014, presented in "The Human Era @ Work: Findings from the Energy Project and *Harvard Business Review*," 2014, PDF link available at Karyn Twaronite, "A Global Survey on the Ambiguous State of Employee Trust," *Harvard Business Review*, July 22, 2016, https://hbr.org/2016/07/a-global-survey-on-the-ambiguous-state-of-employee-trust#. Emphasis added.

4. Eric Garton and Michael Mankins, "Engaging Your Employees Is Good, but Don't Stop There," *Harvard Business Review*, December 9, 2015, https://hbr.org/2015/12/engaging-your-employees-is-good-but-dont-stop-there.

5. Gordon Tredgold, "29 Surprising Facts That Explain Why Millennials See the World Differently," *Inc.*, May 2, 2016, https://www.inc.com/gordon-tredgold/29-surprising-facts-about-millennials-and-what-motivates-them.html.

6. Larry Fink, "A Sense of Purpose" (annual letter to CEOs, World Economic Forum, Davos, Switzerland, 2018), BlackRock, https://www.blackrock.com/hk/en/insights/larry-fink-ceo-letter.

7. From Hawking's speech that he wrote for his seventieth birthday, quoted in Alok Jha, "Stephen Hawking Marks 70th Birthday with Speech to Leading Cosmologists," *Guardian*, January 8, 2012, https://www.theguardian.com/science/2012/jan/08/stephen-hawking-70-cambridge-speech.

Chapter 9: Savannah Bananas

1. Zach Spedden, "Sophomore Year a Success for Savannah Bananas," Ballpark Digest, August 29, 2017, https://ballparkdigest.com/2017/08/29/sophomore-year-a-success-for-savannah-bananas/.

2. Spedden, "Sophomore Year a Success."

3. Jesse Cole, *Find Your Yellow Tux: How to Be Successful by Standing Out* (Austin, TX: Lioncrest, 2017).

Chapter 10: The Emotion Imperative

1. Diana Ransom, "How Dollar Shave Club Rode a Viral Video to Sales Success," *Inc.*, July/August 2015, https://www.inc.com/magazine/201507/diana-ransom/how-youtube-crashed-our-website.html.

2. Sameet Gupte, "A New Kind of Currency: The Emotion Economy," Raconteur, November 1, 2017, https://www.raconteur.net/technology/a-new-kind-of-currency-the-emotion-economy.

3. Gupte, "A New Kind of Currency."

4. Alan S. Cowen and Dacher Keltner, "Self-Report Captures 27 Distinct Categories of Emotion Bridged by Continuous Gradients," *PNAS* 114, no. 38 (September 2017): E7900–E7909.

ABOUT THE AUTHOR

Mark Sanborn is president of Sanborn & Associates, Inc., an idea studio dedicated to developing leaders in business and in life. Mark is an international bestselling author and noted expert on leadership, team building, customer service, and change. Mark's clients include Costco, FedEx, Harley Davidson, ESPN, and other well-known brand-name organizations. He is an accomplished speaker and leader, and former president of the National Speakers Association.

HAVE MARK SANBORN BRING *THE INTENTION IMPERATIVE* TO LIFE AT YOUR NEXT MEETING OR CONFERENCE.

For more information and videos showing how Mark will educate and entertain your audience with his timely solutions, customized for your industry and goals, please contact his office directly at (303) 683-0714 or visit www.MarkSanborn.com.

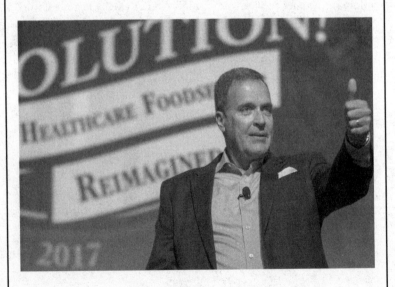

For more information about coaching, consulting, and training, visit marksanborn.com/assessment to get your free assessment.